ISLAND
vegan

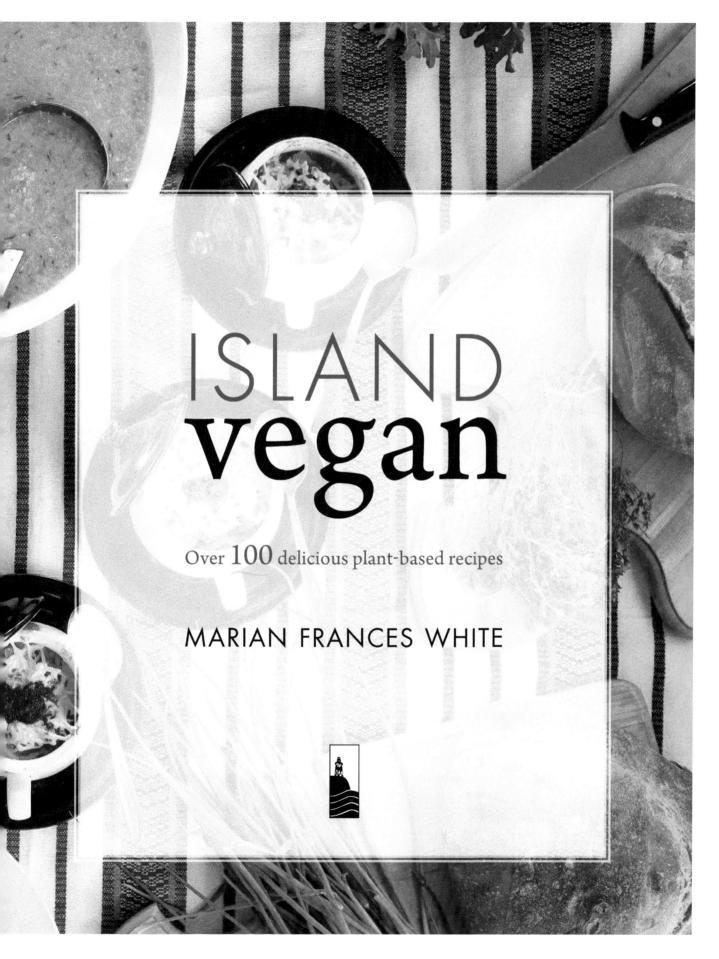

ISLAND
vegan

Over **100** delicious plant-based recipes

MARIAN FRANCES WHITE

BREAKWATER
P.O. BOX 2188, ST. JOHN'S, NL, CANADA, A1C 6E6
WWW.BREAKWATERBOOKS.COM

ISBN 978-1-55081-765-2
COPYRIGHT © 2019 Marian Frances White
FOOD PHOTOGRAPHY Jackson McLean

Second Printing

A CIP catalogue record for this book is available from Library and Archives Canada.

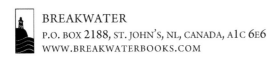

We acknowledge the financial support of the Government of Canada and the Government of Newfoundland and Labrador through the Department of Tourism, Culture, Industry and Innovation for our publishing activities. PRINTED AND BOUND IN CANADA.

Breakwater Books is committed to choosing papers and materials for our books that help to protect our environment. To this end, this book is printed on a recycled paper and other controlled sources that are certified by the Forest Stewardship Council®.

The information provided in Island Vegan *represents personal opinion and experience and does not replace professional medical or nutritional advice. Always consult your physician or a health-care professional before starting any nutrition or exercise program to determine if it is right for you.*

DEDICATED TO

My sweet grandchildren,

Ella Sophie, Mila Josephine, and Miko Sebastian Doelle.

I could never prepare a dish

as perfect as you three.

contents

acknowledgments

Over the years and decades, I have prepared numerous meals with family and friends and thank them for their support and encouragement with *Island Vegan*. Special thanks to Beni Malone, who has always been my closest taste tester, an excellent life companion, and my right hand in the kitchen—not to mention an avid forager of all things edible, especially chanterelle mushrooms, wild blueberries, and plumboys, or blackberries as most people call them. Like their mother, Anahareo, my grandchildren Ella, Mila, and Miko are also proving to be enthusiastic in the kitchen. Their discerning taste buds inspire me to create food that is as close to nature's intention as possible. Marco, their father, has brought a whole new level of appreciation of fresh, tasty foods with plenty of herbs and spices to our table. We are so thankful they all live on this island. Thanks to my niece, Amelia White, who helped compile a portion of the first draft, and to my niece, Noelle Malone, who helped measure and test many of these revised recipes. Thanks to my goddaughter, Zoe Cleland, who tested and tasted recipes in the dessert section. And thanks to Ann Gibson for helping on pie-making day. Dash Malone has always been a food enthusiast, and here's a huge amount of gratitude for your positive approach to food preparation and to life in general. Thank you and much appreciation to Naeme and Greg, who are not only amazing vegan cooks, but have helped prepare numerous meals in my kitchen. Their pesto and sunflower yogurt are lovingly featured here. In fact, when the pressure is on, there is no better person in the kitchen than Naeme, so an extra huge thank you to my sister for all her food preparing while creating this cookbook and TLC along the way.

Special thanks to Jackson McLean for his wonderful photographs. Having a vegan photographer was a dream come true.

Extra special thanks to Rebecca Rose for publishing *Island Vegan*, and to Rhonda Molloy, Breakwater's designer, for superb attention to detail. Thank you, James Langer, for your meticulous editorial eye.

I am thrilled to release *Island Vegan*, a celebration of my forty-plus years as a vegan. Back in the mid-1990s, I published *The Eldamar Cookbook: A Fine Vegan Cuisine*. In that edition, I laid out my path to becoming a vegan, something that was not as trendy or as socially acceptable as it is today. However, my quest and approach to health as outlined twenty-five years ago, when I was a fledgling vegetarian in remote Newfoundland, is still relevant today.

Ever since I became a strict vegetarian in the mid-1970s, I have attempted to create meals that are both nutritionally satisfying and pleasing to the palate. During this time, I have also been fortunate to have enjoyed many delicious dinners and desserts prepared by other people. Some of their recipes are celebrated in these pages.

My first cooking experiences (outside of my parents' kitchen) were as a teenager in the Carleton University cafeteria in Ottawa. Every weekend, I subsidized my journalism school fees by cooking huge amounts of food for students who lived in the residences at Carleton. A year later, when my curiosity took me to Canada's west coast, I subsidized my meagre writing earnings with a part-time job as a chef at a youth hostel in Vancouver. There I had to conceal my vegetarianism in order to get and maintain that job. Years later while spending several months in Jamaica, I absorbed the wise words of the Rastafarian philosopher, Maurice, as he conjured up Ital Coconut Soup and spoke of the cosmic connections between islands, especially Newfoundland and Jamaica.

Many of the recipes contained here were born out of necessity. When I became a vegetarian, there were few recipe books to consult, and obtaining special ingredients was no easy task. There were many awkward moments as I explained that I did not eat anything from the animal kingdom, which included fish, eggs, or any form of dairy products. Few believed I could survive, let alone thrive. I read whatever I could find on vegetarianism and later enrolled at Hippocrates Health Institute in Boston. There I spent several months studying this alternative lifestyle. Besides not eating from the animal kingdom, I began a holistic approach to my life, practicing yoga, reflexology, studying herbs, and familiarizing myself with the new concept of deep breathing and being relaxed and in touch with my body. In 2013, I became a certified reflexology therapist.

I once wrote in a poem, "everything changes but there is nothing new," and I realize this is significant when it comes to cooking. For example, when I embarked on a raw foods diet in the '70s, it was called just that—*raw food cooking*. Today, a raw foods diet is caught up in the plant-based, slow-cooking food movement. Whatever way you term it, this is a reference to food prepared with little or no deep frying, over boiling, or drowning in sauces that mask the vegetables, but rather food eaten in its raw and natural state or lightly slow cooked. Over the years, I have devised a vegetarian diet for a northern climate: one that is a combination of raw fruits and vegetables, as well as sprouts, nuts, and vegetables, and a wide variety of cooked foods that include grains, pastas, and legumes. I continue to enjoy daily salads with tasty dressings, but I also eat baked goods and cooked organic food grown and prepared close to home.

The rewards of vegan cooking helped keep me on a healthy path but have also brought me to places I dreamed of going. Several years ago, through a good friend of mine, Debbie Petite, I met her cousin, Jerry Petite, who at that time lived in Mallorca, Spain—an island I had always wanted to visit. Before the end of our first conversation, Jerry offered me a stay at his apartment in the city of Palma de Mallorca. I asked him if he was in the habit of offering his home to perfect strangers. His response surprised me: "You are not a stranger to me.

I'm vegetarian and I often cook from your cookbook. I would be happy to have you prepare food in my kitchen, just wish I could be there to eat it too." That winter, Beni and I spent a wonderful month feasting from the market in Mallorca and preparing great meals in Jerry's kitchen.

I resolved to publish *Island Vegan* several years ago after I received an email from a woman in New York who told me she had raised her daughter on *Eldamar*. Now that her daughter was going away to college, she wanted to give her a copy to guide her through her college years. Sadly, I did not have one extra copy I could send, nor did I have it available digitally. That will change with this publication, thanks to Breakwater Books. The other change is that Beni and I are now proud grandparents to Ella, Mila, and Miko. I so look forward to having this cookbook smudged by them while making cookies or smoothies.

One of the great rewards of my vegetarian lifestyle is the mind and body focus on personal health that has come over these forty years living as a vegan. Not to say there are not many other factors to living a healthy, productive life, but I have always maintained that my path to health has been paved with tasty vegan meals.

What I have added in *Island Vegan* are suggestions that will help you use this cookbook wisely. Most of my recipes are wheat-free: almond, spelt, rice, coconut, and pea flour are mainstays in my kitchen. If you have a severe allergy to wheat, you will want to avoid spelt and corn flour altogether and use a combination of rice, coconut, or potato flour.

My biggest challenge in compiling this cookbook has been to be precise about my recipes. I am known to add a pinch of this and a dab of that at the last minute. I am also known to revise recipes that were seemingly perfect. So I encourage you to experiment with these recipes and adjust the ingredients to suit your own taste. Most of all, enjoy the rewards of vegan dining.

Marian Frances White, 2019

substitutes

eggs

To replace eggs, you have several choices. You can use a commercially produced, powdered egg substitute that is wheat and gluten free. This popular product is made from guar gum, cornstarch, and baking powder, and 1 tbsp + ⅛ cup of water = 1 egg. However, there are other substitutes that work great too.

A half cup of applesauce per egg works as an excellent substitute in pancakes. For cakes use additional baking powder.

One small ripe banana (½ cup mashed) per egg also works great in baked goods. If you do not want the taste of banana in everything, try chia seeds or ground flax meal. When using flax meal or chia, combine with water (1 tbsp + ⅛ cup of water). Stir and let stand in a bowl for a few minutes while you measure the other ingredients for your baking.

When my daughter, Anahareo, was a child, I most often used arrowroot starch to thicken jellies, sauces, or jams in place of cornstarch. Today I still use arrowroot. I find it has no lingering flavour, does not colour the food, and is a perfect thickening agent. Mix 1 tbsp with ⅛ cup cold water per each cup of jam or jelly.

milk

My favourite milk is unsweetened coconut milk. However, I also use hemp, rice, almond, and occasionally soy. Coconut milk or yogurt is great in Asian dishes, whereas almond is a thinner milk and better used in baking.

For *vegenaise* spread, I only use soy milk, simply because it thickens best. I also prefer organic soy milk in chai tea or latte. If you want a richer taste, try hot coconut milk. All the milks I use are unsweetened and as organic as possible.

baking powder, yeast, and oil

Use aluminum-free baking powder: Avoid aluminum in every aspect of your

life, especially when heating food or even applying deodorant; it clogs pores and is a carcinogen.

Nutritional Yeast Flakes:
Not to be confused with dry, active yeast used in breads, or brewer's yeast that is less tasty and somewhat bitter. Made from deactivated yeast found in molasses, it is then dried and heated. High in B-12, vitamins and minerals, this yeast adds a cheesy flavour to tossed salad, and is yummy on fresh popped, organic popcorn.

Oil: For any recipe that calls for butter you can use a health-brand vegan spread, like Earth Balance soy-free spread. My favourite oils are coconut and sunflower for baking and avocado for cooking. Olive oil is great in salad dressings but should not be heated.

fruit salads, drinks, & smoothies

1 organic red delicious apple, diced

1 perfectly ripe banana, diced

1 cup cubed fresh pineapple

½ cup raisins (soaked the night before)

1 orange, cubed

2 tsp lemon juice

juice of 1 orange

red seedless grapes

fall into the bowl fruit salad

Combine the apple, banana, and pineapple. Add the raisins and orange cubes. Mix together with the lemon and orange juice. Garnish with grapes.

SUGGESTED TOPPING Coconut yogurt or fresh coconut cream (page 24).

a winter's breakfast for two

4 to 6 organic apricots

½ cup organic seedless raisins

1 red delicious apple

1 banana

Boston seed yogurt or any non-dairy yogurt

Soak the apricots and raisins in spring water overnight.

In the morning, grate the apple and slice the banana into a bowl. Drain the apricots and raisins (reserve the juice!) and add them to the bowl.

Top each serving with a heaping tablespoon of Boston Seed Yogurt (page 54) or any non-dairy yogurt. Pour a little of the juice from the soaked fruit over the yogurt.

> ↳ **WHEN GRATING** apples, unless you want applesauce, use the grating surface with the wider holes. Apples oxidize quickly after grating, and this is what makes the apple turn brown so quickly. So serve immediately and enjoy a truly comforting winter's breakfast, any time of the year.

wild as the hills blueberry juice

16 cups of spring water

8 cups of fresh (or frozen) blueberries

½ cup of Quebec maple syrup

In a large stainless-steel pot, bring the spring water to a boil.

Add blueberries, bring to a boil, reduce heat, and simmer for 20 minutes.

Allow to cool in the pot for about 1 hour. Use a colander to strain the juice into a bowl, press the pulp to extract all the juice, and then add the maple syrup to the liquid.

Bottle in sterilized bottles and refrigerate.

HINT: The juice keeps well in the fridge for up to 1 week. You can freeze the juice too, but leave enough room in the jar for the juice to expand—about ¾ full.

watermelon drink

1 medium watermelon

½ cup spring water (approx.)

Slice and remove the rind from the watermelon. In a blender, blend the red pulp and seeds for 1 minute (seeds aid digestion). Add the spring water and blend for 1 minute.

Slowly pour the blended melon through a strainer into a medium-sized bowl. Press with a large spoon to separate the juice from the pulp. This should make about 4 cups of tasty watermelon juice. You can store the remaining juice in the fridge for up to three days, so enjoy it sooner rather than later.

MELON IS said to be a body-cleansing, detoxing food. It is best eaten alone early in the morning since it digests quickly. Drink slowly and savour every mouthful.

2 cups coconut or almond milk (almond is thinner)

1 cup fresh or frozen blueberries

4 ice cubes (omit if blueberries are frozen)

⅛ cup pure maple syrup

1 ripe banana

lavender shake up

Blend all ingredients for 2 minutes or until smooth and creamy.

The colour rivals the taste, but together, what a combination!

vanilla shakes a winter's night

2 cups unsweetened coconut milk

1 tsp organic vanilla

2 tbsp hemp hearts

2 tbsp pure maple syrup

1 ripe banana with speckles

1 cup organic strawberries or raspberries

Blend all the ingredients for 2 minutes and serve immediately.

🌱 MOST BERRIES have seeds, so if you want a very smooth shake, pour through a sieve or colander.

Beni's plumboy shake

2 cups coconut milk

1 cup fresh plumboys (blackberries)

¼ cup vegan protein powder

½ cup coconut yogurt

Blend all ingredients for 2 minutes, strain to remove the seeds, and serve fresh.

🌱 FOR THIS delicious shake, it's pretty important to strain through a sieve.

like nuts milk

1 cup almonds

½ cup walnuts

2½ cups spring water

1 cup coconut milk

1 tbsp chia seeds

1 tbsp pure maple syrup (optional)

Rinse the nuts before use and soak for about 2 hours in 2 cups of the spring water. Drain water from the nuts and add them to a blender with remaining ½ cup spring water and 1 cup of coconut milk. Blend for 2 minutes or until creamy. Add the chia seeds and blend for another minute.

For a sweet milk, add the maple syrup and blend.

Strain through a sieve for a smooth milk.

🌱 THIS NUT milk is great as a power brain booster. Or use it on granola or in any dessert recipe.

coconut cream Jamaican style

1 block (10 oz) pure coconut cream

¼ cup pure maple syrup

1 fresh coconut

HINT: Coconut shells make great bird feeders. In our climate, it might take a lifetime to compost. However, the pulp of the coconut will compost much faster.

SHORT METHOD

Melt the pure coconut cream in a saucepan with just enough water to keep coconut from sticking to the pan. Stir constantly. When melted and smooth, sweeten with maple syrup.

For an even shorter method, use coconut whipped cream, available in the frozen section of new food markets.

LONG METHOD (BUT THE REAL THING)
AS TAUGHT TO ME BY MAURICE LYNCH IN NEGRIL, JAMAICA

Insert a stainless-steel kitchen spike into the top holes of the coconut to drain the coconut water (about 1 cup in each coconut). Drink this water fresh.

Next, break open the coconut's outer shell with a hammer. Maurice would hold the coconut firmly in one hand and whack the coconut with his machete. With the pointed blade of a knife, extract the flesh of the coconut from the shell and compost the shell.

Soak the extracted pieces of coconut in warm water for 15 minutes. With a sharp paring knife, peel the brown skin from the fleshy coconut.

Rinse the remaining white coconut pieces. Put the white coconut through a juicer that will separate the pulp from the rest of the coconut. What gets extracted is pure coconut cream.

Of course, Maurice did not have a juicer. He would grate each coconut piece, soak the pulp in warm water for a few minutes, and strain the pulp through a mesh cloth. I use an old-fashioned Champion juicer that has an attachment which separates the pulp from the cream, the same method you would use to make fresh carrot juice.

This recipe takes patience, but there is no taste like it, and no need to add anything else. Serve over your dessert or use in Ital Soup (page 60).

soy cream

¾ cup chilled soy milk

1 cup sunflower or other light oil

1 tbsp fresh lemon juice

¼ cup pure maple syrup

1 tsp organic vanilla

Pour the soy milk into a food processor. Add the oil slowly, blending on a low setting for a minute, then increase the speed until a thick cream forms. It can take up to 1½ cups of oil. Add the lemon juice, maple syrup, and vanilla. Chill before serving over dessert.

banana ice cream

4 ripe (speckled) bananas

CAROB SAUCE

1 tbsp of carob

2 tbsp water

2 tbsp pure maple syrup

Peel the bananas and place in an air-tight plastic bag. Stick a straw in the corner of the open end of the bag and draw out the air before sealing the bag. Place in freezer for at least 8 hours.

Remove from freezer bags and funnel each banana through a juicer (be sure the blade is set for smooth extraction) into cones. One banana per cone.

Serve as is or dipped in carob sauce.

CAROB SAUCE

Hand mix the carob with the water until smooth. Add the maple syrup and whisk.

🌿 **MY OLD-FASHIONED** Champion juicer makes the best banana ice cream.

vegetable cocktail party

6 medium carrots

1 beet, scrubbed not peeled

2 stalks celery

2 cored apples

1 tbsp fresh ginger stem (optional)

Almost any combination of vegetables can be juiced together or used separately.

Wash all vegetables thoroughly before juicing. Use organic vegetables whenever possible; however, most chemicals are extracted in the pulp, leaving you with a pure organic juice.

Put carrots, beet, celery, apples, and ginger stem (if you like ginger) through a vegetable juicer. Strain through cheese cloth or mesh strainer for a smoother drink. Makes about 4 cups.

➤ **DIGESTION BEGINS** in the mouth, so chew your juice and drink your food!

apple to the core
(aka nectar of the goddesses)

2 organic apples

Be sure to wash your apples well.

Using a hand grater, grate apples into a medium-sized, stainless-steel bowl.

Pour into a cheese cloth, and squeeze juice into a wide measuring cup.

Enjoy immediately, and drink slowly.

➤ **IF YOU** must share this drink, use 4 apples.

The making of a good salad begins with the greens that go into it. Salad greens should always be garden fresh and free from chemical sprays. Wash them in cold water, then shake in a cheese-cloth bag or dry in a salad spinner to remove excess moisture. During storage, it's okay to have a slight dampness at the base of your salad greens, but too much moisture will make your salad wet and unappealing in the bowl. Use a wide variety of greens from lettuce, young dandelion greens, spinach, chicory leaves, beet tops, cabbage, and sprouts. Sliced radish, shredded carrots, or beet add zest and crunch to a dinner salad. Have ready a pair of kitchen scissors for cutting herbs and onion tops.

salads, dressings, & sauces

soyanaise

1 cup chilled soy milk

1 + 1 cup sunflower oil

2 tbsp lemon juice

pinch of pink Himalayan salt

1 tsp dill

1 tsp parsley

Pour chilled soy milk into a food processor or blender. Blend and gradually add 1 cup sunflower oil. Add the lemon juice and salt.

Continue adding oil (up to another cup) until mixture thickens, not unlike regular mayonnaise.

Dress with dill and parsley or use plain and simple. Bottle and chill for immediate use.

Will last up to 1 week in refrigerator.

Anahareo's fave tahini dressing

¼ cup sesame tahini

¾ cup olive oil

2 tbsp apple cider vinegar

¼ cup fresh lemon juice

2 tbsp spring water

1 tbsp prepared mustard

2 cloves garlic, pressed

1 tsp Bragg Liquid Soy Seasoning or pink Himalayan salt

½ tsp finely chopped parsley

Hand whisk the sesame tahini, olive oil, apple cider vinegar, lemon juice, water, and mustard until smooth. Then add the garlic, soy seasoning (or salt), and parsley and blend. Mix until creamy, adding water as needed.

HINT: This dressing will thicken when refrigerated. If too thick, add more oil, or if you want a smoother dressing with a full citrus taste, add more lemon juice.

tossed salad dressing

½ cup olive oil

2 cloves garlic, minced

¼ cup nutritional yeast flakes

1 tbsp Bragg Liquid Soy Seasoning

1 tsp pink Himalayan salt

juice of 1 lemon

2 tbsp Bragg's apple cider vinegar

Prepare your favourite fresh salad in a bowl. Sprinkle in some finely cut herbs (sprig of fresh basil, parsley, thyme, and dill).

With a wooden salad spoon and fork, toss the olive oil through your salad. Then add the garlic, yeast flakes, liquid soy seasoning, and salt. Toss again. Pour the lemon juice and apple cider vinegar over the salad. Toss again and serve.

1 cup fresh parsley (stems removed)

½ cup spring water

4 cloves garlic

1 cup olive oil

¼ cup fresh lemon juice

1 tbsp Bragg Liquid Soy Seasoning

1 tbsp nutritional yeast

1 tbsp sweet mustard

parsley garlic cleansing dressing

Blend parsley and spring water for 1 minute. Then add the remaining ingredients and blend for another minute or until smooth.

This is a thick, creamy dressing to toss through your salad.

8 oz soft tofu

¼ cup spring water

¼ cup fresh lemon juice

½ cup sunflower oil

1 tbsp dill

1 tsp pink Himalayan salt

1 tbsp Bragg Liquid Soy Seasoning
or gluten-free organic soy sauce

1 tsp fresh cut parsley

showy tofu dressing

Blend all the ingredients for 2 minutes and serve.

This is a thick, filling dressing to complement any salad.

colour therapy dressing

8 oz soft tofu

½ cup pure water

¾ cup olive oil

¼ cup pickled beet juice or
¼ cup grated beet and
juice of 1 lemon

½ cup chopped red onion

1 tsp dill

1 tsp basil

1 tbsp Bragg Liquid Soy
Seasoning or pink Himalayan salt

½ tsp horseradish powder or
hot mustard

Blend the tofu, water, olive oil, and pickled beet juice for 1 minute. Then add the remaining ingredients and blend for a thick, creamy dressing.

pesto the besto

6 cups fresh cleaned basil leaves,
remove part of the stem

6 cloves garlic

2 cups olive oil

1 tbsp pink Himalayan salt

½ cup fresh pine nuts (optional)

In a food processor or blender combine the basil, garlic, olive oil, and salt and blend until creamy (about 2 minutes). You can choose to add the pine nuts to the blender, but remember that pine nuts can go rancid easily and can ruin your precious pesto, so only add pine nuts when making fresh pesto to be served immediately with a particular dish.

Store pesto in small, sterilized Mason jars. Pesto can be frozen and used at your leisure. When freezing, fill jars ¾ full and do not lock the jar too tightly until the contents have frozen. This pesto is especially delicious served over fresh pasta.

southern bell guacamole

1 large, ripe avocado
or 2 small ones

juice of 1 lime

2 cloves garlic, crushed

¼ cup finely chopped bell pepper

1 medium tomato, diced

¼ cup finely chopped red onion

½ tsp cayenne pepper

1 tsp pink Himalayan salt

Slice your avocado in half, remove the pit, spoon the flesh from the peel, and compost the peel. In a stainless-steel bowl, mash the avocado until no lumps appear. Add the remaining ingredients and mix together well. Serve as an appetizer with organic corn chips.

> **AN AVOCADO** is ripe when the peel bends slightly to the touch, but is not too soft, which indicates it is overripe. There is nothing as satisfying as a perfectly ripe avocado, so no point in using one that is over or under ripe.

humus in a flash

3 cups cooked organic chickpeas

4 to 6 cloves garlic

½ cup sesame tahini

juice of 2 fresh lemons

1 tbsp pink Himalayan salt

½ cup olive oil

¼ cup fresh parsley

Blend the chickpeas, garlic, tahini, lemon juice, salt, and olive oil until nice and creamy, about 3 minutes.

Add the parsley and blend again for only 30 seconds.

➤ **TASTY AS** a dip with organic corn chips or rice crackers or on a humus sandwich with pea sprouts.

rocky island west coast salsa

3 cups fresh, chopped organic tomatoes

2 tbsp olive oil

2 tbsp wheat-free tamari soy sauce

3 cloves garlic

1 cup minced onion

½ cup finely diced green pepper

½ tsp chili powder

1 tbsp cumin

1 tsp pink Himalayan salt

½ tbsp coriander

½ tsp cayenne

½ tsp freshly ground black pepper

Blend the tomatoes, olive oil, tamari soy sauce, and garlic lightly for 30 seconds. Remove from blender and pour into a bowl.

Add the onion, green pepper, chili powder, cumin, salt, coriander, cayenne, and black pepper. Mix well.

Enjoy with organic corn chips. Bottle any remaining salsa and keep in refrigerator for up to 1 week.

chlorophyll garden salad

1 head crisp Boston lettuce

1 tsp chives

1 tsp basil

1 tsp garlic

1 tsp thyme

1 carrot, finely grated

2 vine-ripened tomatoes, quartered

½ perfectly ripe avocado, diced

Wash and prepare your lettuce. Toss in the herbs then add the carrot, tomatoes, and avocado.

Serve with Tossed Salad Dressing (page 33).

summer potato salad

8 medium-size new potatoes

2 beets, cooked, skinned and cubed

1 cup sliced mushrooms

1 medium onion, diced

1 medium cucumber, peeled and cut paper thin

½ cup parsley, chopped fine

⅔ cup olive oil

⅓ cup apple cider vinegar

1 tbsp Dijon mustard

1 tsp pink Himalayan salt

½ tsp kelp power

1 cup soyanaise (page 32)

pinch fresh dill

pepper to taste

Scrub the potatoes and leave the skins on. Steam them until they are soft enough that a fork easily inserts through the potato. Remove from heat, peel off skin, and cube.

Steam the beets whole for 60 minutes. Pinch off the skins and cube.

In a single bowl, combine the cooked potatoes and beets with the mushrooms, onion, cucumber, parsley, olive oil, apple cider vinegar, mustard, salt, kelp powder, and pepper. Mix ½ cup soyanaise throughout the salad. Top with remaining soyanaise and garnish with dill. Chill in the refrigerator for at least 1 hour and serve.

HINT: Beets are cooked when the peel is easily pinched off.

[summer potato salad]

Caesar salad

1 large head organic romaine
lettuce

2 tsp lemon juice

¼ cup olive oil

1 tbsp Bragg Liquid Soy
Seasoning

1 clove garlic, crushed

½ cup rice parmesan cheese

¼ cup soyanaise (page 32)

½ cup croutons

CROUTONS

3 slices not-so-fresh rice or
spelt bread

3 tbsp olive oil

2 cloves garlic, crushed

1 tsp pink Himalayan salt

Thoroughly wash and drain your lettuce, tear pieces into a
salad bowl.

In a separate bowl, whisk the lemon juice, olive oil, liquid soy
seasoning, garlic, rice parmesan, and soyanaise.

Toss these mixed seasonings throughout the lettuce and then
add croutons.

CROUTONS

Preheat oven to 350°F.

Three slices of bread will make 1 cup of croutons. Cut the
bread in ½-inch cubes. Toss in a bowl with olive oil and garlic.
Sprinkle with salt. Spread over a baking sheet and bake for 30
minutes.

half-moon bean salad

1½ cups cooked kidney beans

1 cup cooked chickpeas

1 cup cooked green string beans, cut in 1-inch pieces

½ cup finely chopped celery

½ cup thinly sliced red onion half-moons

½ cup olive oil

2 tbsp apple cider vinegar

1 tsp organic Dijon mustard

½ tsp pink Himalayan salt

pinch ground black pepper

Combine the beans, chickpeas, string beans, celery, and onions in a salad bowl. Lightly toss in the olive oil, vinegar, mustard, salt, and pepper.

HINT: This salad gets even tastier if refrigerated for a day or so. The cool temperature allows the various flavours to be absorbed by the beans.

healing coleslaw

1 small cabbage, sliced in quarters

1 medium carrot

1 medium beet

2 tsp Bragg Liquid Soy Seasoning

¼ cup fresh lemon juice (or more if you like a sharper taste)

4 cloves garlic, minced

¼ cup olive oil

½ cup soyanaise (page 32)

Remove the outer leaves of cabbage and store for use in cabbage rolls. Cut out the center core of the cabbage. I like to munch on this raw center while I prepare my coleslaw.

Finely grate the cabbage, carrot, and beet. Add the remaining ingredients and toss together. Serve fresh.

HINT: To save time, you can use a food processor, but be careful not to over blend or the coleslaw will be too creamy.

sprout salads

Sprouts are an inexpensive food source. They are easy to grow at home and give a constant source of fresh, nutritious food all year round. They like to grow in a cool environment, so winter sprouting is a healthy way to go. Thankfully, they are often available at good nutrition stores and at farmers' markets.

Sprouts are great eaten on their own, as healthy additions to any salad, or on an avocado or humus sandwich. Always use fresh sprouts that are rinsed and drained daily to maintain their freshness. Refrigerate once sprouted and use within 2 to 3 days.

All unhulled seeds and beans—like alfalfa, mung beans, peas, and even lentils—can be sprouted. When these foods germinate, they produce proteins, vitamins, and minerals.

CONTINUES ▶

how to grow your own sprouts

To sprout any seed, wash and soak overnight in a large Mason jar or other large jar. The example below uses alfalfa seeds.

DAY 1

→ Wash ¼ cup of alfalfa seeds and drain off the water.

→ Place the seeds in a Mason jar.

→ Add 2 cups of water and soak overnight.

DAY 2

→ Place a thin wire mesh over the mouth of the jar and secure with an elastic band.

→ Place the jar in your sink and rinse the seeds thoroughly by allowing cool water to pour into the jar and run over the rim into the sink.

→ Turn upside down and drain.

→ Keep the jar in an angled upside-down resting position for the coming days. You may need a tray under the jar to capture excess water. Air must circulate, so don't block off the flow of air. Cover the exterior of the jar with a cloth during this sprouting period.

→ Turn upright and rinse, as before, twice daily. Repeat watering for the rest of the week. Always keep sprouting seeds in a cool location.

→ In 1 week, your jar will be full of sprouts.

→ The sprouts must be cleaned (instructions below) and put in the light to gain chlorophyll before ingesting.

cleaning method

→ Pour the sprouts from the Mason jar directly into a large stainless-steel bowl.

→ Clean jar thoroughly and set aside.

→ Fill bowl with cold water. The hulls or tops of the seeds will rise to the top of the bowl (or most of them will). Pull these hulls to one side of the bowl and remove to compost.

→ Gently stir sprouts in the water again and even more hulls will rise to the top.

→ Take the cleaned sprouts from the water, returning to the large Mason jar.

CONTINUES ▶

- → Cover once again with mesh and turn upside down. This will drain excess water.
- → Place in sunny location.
- → Rinse once a day.
- → Do not cover the jar with a cloth as they now need light to gain chlorophyll.
- → Within two days, the tips of the sprouts will turn green. Rinse once a day.
- → They are now ready to enjoy on a salad or sandwich.
- → Store in refrigerator or in a very cool room.

Hippocrates rejuvelac

This fermented grain liquid is used as the fermenting agent in making seed yogurt.

Rejuvelac is high in B vitamins and also has vitamin C and K. If you are wheat sensitive, you can most often digest this naturally fermented liquid; otherwise, try rice as your grain.

1 cup wheat berries

3 cups water

FERMENTED FOODS should be used with reservation by persons with overly acidic stomachs. However, while the evidence is anecdotal, many people with sensitive stomachs find the probiotic activity of rejuvelac to be soothing to the stomach and intestines.

Use soft wheat berries. Wash berries well. Combine the berries and water in a large Mason jar. Cover loosely with the lid on. Be sure to cover the entire jar with a cloth to keep out light. Soak at room temperature for 48 hours. When the water has a sweet fermented smell (not sour) pour the liquid off and use as rejuvelac. Store any rejuvelac you don't use in the refrigerator.

Add 2 more cups of water to berries and let soak again for 24 hours—pour off the rejuvelac to use as a digestive-aid drink or in seed yogurt recipes. This is the peak day for the highest vitamin and enzyme content. Rejuvelac acquires a strong taste after the second and third day. It's time to compost the wheat berries and start a new batch.

Use the rejuvelac in Boston Seed Yogurt (page 54).

Boston seed yogurt

2 cups hulled and ground sunflower seeds

1 cup ground almonds

rejuvelac (page 53)

Grind the seeds and almonds separately in a coffee grinder or hand grinder. Then combine and add enough rejuvelac to make the consistency of pancake batter.

Pour this smooth, creamy sauce into a glass jar (no aluminum or plastic) with a lid. Cover loosely (a plate or bowl on top will do). Set in a warm place for 6 to 8 hours. Ideal temperature is 75°F to 100°F or 25° to 35°C. An electric yogurt maker works well; although, a covered glass jar in the sun or on a hot-water radiator works just as well.

When the sauce is fermented, "whey" will sink to the bottom of the container. Stir the "whey" into the yogurt because it contains valuable enzymes and vitamins.

Chill before serving. Delicious with A Winter's Breakfast for Two (page 19).

THIS YOGURT is hardcore, and it might take a few attempts before you get it right. But it's worth it, since so many commercially produced yogurts are "enhanced" with sweeteners and preservatives. While the taste of Boston Seed Yogurt is unique and sharp, it should not be sour. If it is, your rejuvelac is over fermented. I generally only make this yogurt in wintertime, when the temperature can be more easily controlled.

J ust as it is better to steam vegetables rather than boil them, don't destroy the life of your soup by boiling or overcooking it. Yes, you will need to bring your soup to a boil, but then simmer the soup until the ingredients are cooked, leaving vegetables a little chewy rather than mush.

Always wash grains and vegetables before adding to soup stock.

Use the steaming water from vegetables for your soup stock. It is full of vitamins.

To avoid getting gas from beans, discard the water you soak the beans in before you add them to the soup stock.

Soup pots vary in size and shape. I typically only use stainless-steel pots that hold about twelve cups of stock. The main point is for the pot to have a thick bottom to prevent burning. I like a pot with a round base and deep, straight sides and a cover. I also find handles on both sides essential to handling hot soup easily. However, for some soups, when I cook with lentils, I generally use cast iron to enhance the natural iron contained in this legume. Cast iron lasts forever and will not crack. I still use my mother's, so it can be passed on through generations.

soups

leek and potato coconut soup

2 tbsp coconut oil

1 large onion, diced

4 cups of washed and chopped leeks

4 large potatoes, chopped small

2 cubes organic vegetable bouillon

2 cups water

2 cups coconut milk

1 frozen cube of parsley or
1 tbsp of finely cut fresh parsley

½ tsp fresh-ground black pepper

In a deep cast-iron or stainless-steel pot, heat oil and sauté onion until golden, not browned.

Add chopped leeks and potatoes and cook on medium heat for 5 minutes.

Dissolve the vegetable bouillon in the water then stir into the pot and simmer for 20 minutes. Leave lid on loosely, and stir occasionally.

Remove from heat, and with a hand masher, pulse everything in the pot. Add coconut milk and stir. If you prefer a smoother soup, pour into food processor and blend for 2 minutes. Otherwise it is perfect as is.

Return soup to stovetop and heat to a bubble. Toss in the parsley.

Grind a sprinkle of fresh black pepper over each bowl before serving.

Serve with warm bread or buns.

DURING SUMMERTIME, there's plenty of parsley in the garden. But to have parsley available all year round, I make a habit of picking enough to blend with water and freeze in ice-cube trays. Once frozen, they can be stored in jars in the freezer.

Ital soup

A Jamaican dish eaten almost daily by Rastafarian followers. Revised for a northern climate and stock on hand.

6 cups vegetable stock

2 cups unsweetened coconut cream

½ cup diced onion

½ cup diced green or red pepper

1 cup cubed sweet potato

1 cup diced potato

¼ tsp herbs: savory, thyme, and parsley

2 cups chopped spinach or turnip greens

1 tsp cayenne pepper

1 tbsp Bragg Liquid Soy Seasoning

In a stewing pot, bring vegetable stock to a boil. Reduce heat to mediuim-low and add unsweetened coconut cream.

Add the onion, green or red pepper, sweet potato, potato, savory, thyme, and parsley. Simmer for 20 minutes on medium to low heat.

Add the chopped spinach or turnip greens for the last 5 minutes.

Stir in the cayenne pepper and soy seasoning just before serving.

lima bean soup

1 cup lima beans, soaked

1 medium onion, diced

1 stalk celery, finely diced

2 medium potatoes, diced

1 cup diced carrot

1 tsp oregano

1 tsp thyme

2 tbsp brown rice miso paste

2 tbsp Bragg Liquid Soy Seasoning

Soak the lima beans for 2 hours in a large saucepan. Drain, add fresh water, and bring to a boil. Reduce heat to medium-low and cook for 30 minutes until the beans are soft.

Add onion, celery, potatoes, carrot, oregano, thyme, and miso paste. Simmer until vegetables are tender, approximately 20 minutes. Do not overcook.

Add 2 tbsp of liquid soy seasoning to the pot and stir before serving.

zucchini soup

3 medium onions, quartered

¼ cup sunflower oil

3 cloves garlic, minced

1 tbsp cumin

¼ cup vegetable oil

2 medium zucchini

2 cups water

1 cup vegetable stock

¼ cup white rice flour or organic corn flour

2 cups unsweetened coconut milk

A variation of this soup was conjured up by Sandy Morris, way back in the day.

Blend onions and sunflower oil in a food processor for 1 minute. Set aside.

In a deep saucepan or cast-iron pot, lightly sauté the minced garlic and cumin in the vegetable oil on low heat. Then add the blended onions to pot and continue to sauté for 3 minutes until onions are golden, but not browned.

Blend the zucchini in 2 cups of water and add to the pot, returning everything to a boil. Reduce heat and simmer for 10 minutes.

To thicken the soup, hand mix the vegetable stock and white rice flour (or organic corn flour). Stir into the soup and let simmer on low heat.

Gradually add the coconut milk and continue to cook for 5 more minutes.

Serve with a dollop of pesto (page 37) and a sprinkling of fresh dill.

split pea soup

1 cup yellow split peas

6 cups water or vegetable stock

1 bay leaf

1 tbsp miso paste

1 cup chopped onion

1 cup chopped celery with leaves

1 cup diced carrot

1 cup diced turnip

1 cup diced parsnip

2 cups diced potato

pinch of thyme

pinch of sea salt.

fresh-ground black pepper to taste

Add the split peas, water (or stock), and bay leaf to a stainless-steel soup pot and cook for 30 minutes on medium heat until peas are tender. Stir often. Split peas should be soft before adding vegetables, so there's no point in rushing this stage; they simply have to be soft.

Add the miso paste, onion, celery, carrot, turnip, parsnip, and potato and cook for 20 minutes or until tender.

Season with thyme, sea salt, and black pepper. Remove the bay leaf before serving.

For a tasty old-fashioned touch, serve with Dough Balls (page 88).

IF YOU don't have vegetable stock, add 1 organic vegetable bouillon cube to the water that serves as the base of the soup.

hearty lentil stew

1 cup lentils

6 cups vegetable broth

1 cup chopped onion

½ cup celery stalk

1 clove garlic

1 tsp thyme

1 tsp turmeric

1 tbsp vegetable bouillon

1 tsp pink Himalayan salt

1 tbsp miso paste

1 medium carrot

1 medium parsnip

4 medium potatoes

2 cups stewed tomatoes (optional)

2 cups chopped spinach
or 1 cup fresh or frozen organic
peas

Wash the lentils. Bring the broth to a boil and add the lentils. Simmer for 30 minutes over medium heat. Stir occasionally. If you are using sprouted lentils, the cook time is cut to 20 minutes.

Once lentils are soft, add the onion, celery, garlic, thyme, turmeric, vegetable bouillon, salt, miso paste, and continue to simmer on medium to low heat.

Chop the carrot, parsnip, and potatoes and add to them to the pot along with the stewed tomatoes.

After 15 minutes, add the chopped spinach or peas.

Serve with warm soup rolls or Quidi Vidi Road Soup Biscuits (page 92).

stormy red lentil soup

2 cups red lentils, washed

8 cups water

2 onions, chopped

3 potatoes, cubed

2 carrots, sliced

1 parsnip, sliced

1 tsp thyme

1 tbsp Bragg Liquid Soy Seasoning

2 tbsp miso paste

4 tsp pesto or 1 tsp fresh basil

In a large pot, cook the washed red lentils in 4 cups of water. Bring to a boil and then simmer for 20 minutes.

Add the onions, potatoes, carrots, and parsnip. Stir in the thyme, liquid soy seasoning, and miso paste and continue to cook for another 20 minutes, adding the remaining water as the soup thickens.

Top each bowl with 1 tsp of pesto or ¼ tsp of fresh basil.

Great soup for the long, cold, hungry month of March!

bestroni minestrone

1 cup organic corn or rice macaroni

10 cups vegetable broth

2 cloves garlic, diced

1 cup chopped onion

1 cup minced celery

¼ cup parsley

¼ tsp oregano

¼ tsp thyme

¼ tsp basil

⅛ tsp cayenne pepper

1 organic vegetable bouillon cube

3 cups quartered tomatoes

1 cup grated cabbage

1 cup grated carrot

1 cup diced small potato

1 cup diced small parsnip

1 cup cooked and drained organic chickpeas

1 cup cooked and drained organic kidney beans

Measure out your macaroni and set aside.

Bring vegetable broth to a boil in a large pot. Add all remaining ingredients and return to a boil. Reduce heat to medium-low and simmer for 30 minutes. Partially cover and stir occasionally to avoid sticking.

Add macaroni for the last 10 minutes, stirring to ensure it is mixed throughout the soup.

A full meal when served with Dough Balls (page 88).

lunchtime tofu soup for two

1 cup shredded carrot

1 cup diced onion

16 oz medium to firm organic tofu, cut into tiny cubes

1 cup cooked basmati rice

6 cups spring water

1 tsp tarragon

1 tsp basil

1 tsp oregano

1 tbsp Bragg Liquid Soy Seasoning

1 tsp miso paste

½ cup peas

Simmer the carrot, onion, tofu, and cooked basmati rice in the spring water for 15 minutes.

Season with tarragon, basil, and oregano. Lastly, add the bouillon, miso paste, and peas. Simmer for 5 more minutes and serve.

Anahareo's scorpio pumpkin soup

4 cups steamed pumpkin

2 cups vegetable stock or broth

1 onion, diced

¼ cup sunflower oil

1 tsp cumin

1 tsp ginger

2 cloves garlic, minced

½ tsp turmeric

½ tsp coriander

1 tbsp miso paste

2 cups unsweetened coconut milk

1 tbsp pure maple syrup (optional)

Puree the steamed pumpkin in vegetable stock. Set aside.

Sauté the diced onion in sunflower oil. Add the cumin, ginger, garlic, turmeric, coriander, and miso paste.

Pour pureed pumpkin into sautéed onion and spices. Add the coconut milk and cook for 5 minutes.

Optional: Add a dollop of pure maple syrup at the last minute to sweeten this soup.

Serve with a dollop of pesto (page 37) on each bowl.

borscht for Twyla

4 cups shredded raw beet

3 cups shredded raw cabbage

1 cup diced onion

1 cup finely diced celery

6 cups seasoned vegetable broth

2 tsp vegetable bouillon

1 tbsp fresh lemon juice

Place the shredded beet, cabbage, onion, celery, vegetable broth, and vegetable bouillon in a pot and cook (loosely covered) on a medium heat for 30 minutes. Stir to combine flavours.

Remove from heat and add the fresh lemon juice before serving.

> **BORSCHT IS** typically served with a dollop of sour cream. You can use cashew cream or vegan sour cream, which is often available at specialty health-food stores.

full moon corn chowder

3 cups water

2 tbsp avocado or sunflower oil

3 medium potatoes, diced

1 cup diced onion

1 cup medium grated carrot

1 tsp thyme

1 tsp savory

1 tsp celery seed

1 tsp dill

1 tbsp miso or Bragg Liquid Soy Seasoning

3 cups organic corn cut from cob

2 cups unsweetened coconut milk

½ tsp pink Himalayan salt

Bring the water to a boil and set aside.

Heat the oil in large cast-iron pot. Add the onion first, then the thyme, savory, celery seed, and dill. Next add the potatoes, carrot, and miso (or soy seasoning) and simmer for 20 minutes.

Add corn to the pot and continue simmering for another 10 minutes. Then add the coconut milk. If the chowder seems too thick, you can add ½ cup of spring water. Return chowder to a bubble, but do not boil. Stir in salt.

When serving, crack black pepper over each bowl with a dollop of pesto (page 37).

HINT: If you would like a smoother chowder, you can blend the corn in advance.

soup à l'oignon
(french onion soup)

6 medium yellow onions, sliced in thin circles

2 cloves garlic, minced

2 tbsp avocado oil

2 tsp organic corn or yellow chickpea flour

4 cups water

½ tsp thyme

2 tbsp organic vegetable bouillon

¼ cup miso paste

1 cup croutons

1 cup grated non-dairy cheese

In a large cast-iron pot, fry the onions and minced garlic in avocado oil for about 2 minutes until golden, but not brown.

Add the flour and stir until oil is absorbed.

Gradually stir in two cups of water, stirring constantly until no lumps appear. Stir in miso paste until it has dissolved. Then add thyme and bouillon.

Add remaining 2 cups of water and simmer for 10 minutes. Consistency should be creamy but not thick.

Pour equal amounts into oven-proof bowls, about ¾ full, top with croutons and grated dairy-free cheese.

To make croutons see Caesar Salad (page 48).

Broil in the oven for 1 minute until cheese is golden brown. Never leave a dish unattended when broiling.

Serve tout de suite!

breads, muffins, pastries, & pancakes

calm-me-down cinnamon rolls

Yields 24 rolls

1 cup raisins

2 cups warm water

1 tbsp + ½ cup organic coconut sugar

3 tbsp active dry baker's yeast

7 cups unbleached white flour

½ cup organic coconut sugar

1 tsp sea salt

¾ cup sunflower oil

4 tbsp cinnamon

1 cup organic sugar

1 cup crushed walnuts

coconut oil

Soak the raisins in 1 cup warm water for 15 minutes. Set aside.

In a measuring cup, dissolve 1 tbsp organic coconut sugar in 1 cup warm water. Sprinkle the baker's yeast into water. No need to stir. Allow to rise in a sunny location for at least 10-15 minutes. Keep temperature warm and constant until yeast is light and foamy.

Meanwhile, combine the flour, ½ cup organic coconut sugar, and salt in a large mixing bowl. Using a pastry cutter, cut in ¾ cup sunflower oil. Stir in risen yeast. Gradually add ½ cup of raisin water to mixture and sprinkle in 2 tbsp of cinnamon.

Mix and knead dough with your hands for at least 10 minutes, adding a sprinkling of flour as needed to form workable dough. This will keep dough from sticking to the sides of the bowl.

Cover with a cloth and let rise in a warm place until double in bulk, approximately 30 minutes.

Combine 1 cup organic sugar with 2 tbsp cinnamon in a small bowl and set aside.

When dough is double in bulk, sprinkle flour on a wooden table or cutting board and roll dough to 1 inch thickness. Lightly brush the surface of the dough with coconut oil.

Spread a layer of the organic sugar and cinnamon mixture evenly along the dough. Add the soaked and well-drained raisins along with a few crushed walnuts over surface (optional).

Roll dough away from you until one end meets the other. Cut in ¾-inch circles and place on an oiled baking sheet. Buns should lightly touch each other. Brush top of rolls with melted coconut oil. Let rise until almost double in bulk.

Pre-heat oven to 350°F and bake for 30 minutes. While warm, grate coconut cream over rolls. When cool, calmly devour with friends.

extraterrestrial raised doughnuts from Mars

1 cup warm water

2 tbsp maple syrup

3 tbsp active dry baker's yeast

10 cups unbleached white flour

1 tbsp cinnamon

1 tsp nutmeg

2 cups warm but not hot coconut milk

½ cup pure maple syrup

½ cup sunflower oil

2 tbsp egg replacer dissolved in ¼ cup water

1 tsp sea salt

2 tbsp flax meal

4 cups sunflower or organic corn oil

HINT: Before using doughnut cutter, dip cutter into a small bowl of flour before you cut each doughnut. Keep your cutting board lightly floured.

Be sure to have all ingredients ready before you start.

Pour the warm water and maple syrup into a 2-cup measuring cup. Sprinkle yeast on top of sweetened water. Let rise in a warm area of your kitchen until foamy (about 15 minutes).

HINT: You can cover your measuring cup with saran wrap to add warmth to the mixture.

In a food processor or by hand, mix 4 cups of unbleached white flour, cinnamon, nutmeg, warm coconut milk, ½ cup pure maple syrup, sunflower oil, dissolved egg replacer, sea salt, and flax meal. Mix for 1 minute.

Next, pour in the risen yeast and mix for 2 minutes.

Gradually add 4 cups flour to blended mixture until a light dough is formed. Continue to blend for 3 minutes.

In a large mixing bowl, add 2 cups flour and pour in dough from food processor. Use a spatula to scrape dough from sides of processor. Stir together until you have a very stiff dough. Add up to 2 more cups of flour to form a workable dough. Knead for about 10 minutes (it's a real workout!). Dough should be light and bounce back when pressed. Form into a ball and turn over so the round side faces up. Lightly oil top of dough and around edges of your bowl. Cover with a fresh tea cloth and an additional cloth for extra warmth. Let rise in a warm place until double in bulk, about 40 minutes.

Turn dough onto lightly floured board and roll out with a rolling pin to 1 inch thickness. Cut with doughnut cutter and let individual doughnuts rise on a floured board for another 10 minutes.

CONTINUES ▶

GLAZE FOR DOUGHNUTS

1 cup melted dark chocolate

½ cup organic powdered sugar

1 tsp coconut oil

½ tsp pure vanilla

Stir the melted dark chocolate and sugar until creamy. Add coconut oil and vanilla. Dip surface of doughnut into glaze. Allow to cool and serve.

Meanwhile, heat 4 cups of sunflower or organic corn oil in a deep fryer to 375°F.

Using a stainless-steel ladle with holes, drop one doughnut into oil to test for ideal frying temperature. Doughnut should rise to the top of the oil soon after it is placed in the oil. Flip over to fry the other side. Continue to add 4 to 6 doughnuts to your oil at a time.

NOTE: Doughnuts fry quickly! 1½ to 2 minutes on each side is plenty.

Turn onto brown paper or a paper towel to drain off excess oil. Place on a cooling rack and glaze.

spelt pea protein bread

Makes 1 loaf

1 tbsp coconut sugar

1½ cups warm water

3 tbsp active dry baker's yeast

4 cups of coconut milk

3 cups spelt flour

1 tbsp kelp powder

½ cup sunflower oil

½ cup unsulphured blackstrap molasses

2 tbsp egg replacer mixed with ¼ cup water

½ cup pea flour (for additional protein)

Dissolve sugar in warm water. Sprinkle the baker's yeast on top. Stir lightly. Let sit until light and foamy (about 10-15 minutes).

Meanwhile heat 2 cups of coconut milk, do not boil, and pour into a large measuring cup and set aside.

Add 2 cups of the spelt flour to a large bread-making bowl. Stir in the kelp powder. Reserve 1 cup of spelt flour.

Now add the sunflower oil and unsulphered blackstrap molasses to the coconut milk in your large measuring cup. Then add the dissolved egg replacer. Set aside.

Make a volcano or well shape in the middle of the flour mixture. Gradually pour the liquid mixture into the centre of the well. Pour in the risen yeast. Stir with a wooden spoon until all liquid has been absorbed by the flour. Gradually sprinkle the pea flour, ¼ cup at a time, into dough. Work it through the mixture as it will help prevent the dough from sticking to the sides of the bowl.

CONTINUES ▶

2 cups light flour

1 tsp baking powder

1 tsp baking soda

2 tsp ginger powder

1 tsp cinnamon

½ tsp salt substitute or sea salt

½ cup mild flavoured molasses

½ cup coconut sugar

½ cup light oil

1 cup warm coconut milk

¼ cup sesame seeds

vegan butter for spread

Once you have kneaded the dough thoroughly, remove from the bowl and set aside. Clean the bowl, lightly oil the inside, and return dough to the bowl.

Flip dough over and cover with a clean cloth to keep dough warm while rising to double in bulk. This will take approximately 2 hours.

Knead again for several minutes, cover, and allow to rise a second time until double in bulk. This second rising should take 1 hour.

After the second rising, cut off a large slice of dough and form loaves by smoothing and shaping the dough into rounds. Make 2 or 3 rounds for each bread pan and have them touching each other in the pan. Mother always made two rounds.

Place in lightly oiled bread pan—stainless steel, glass, or cast iron preferably

Cover with a cloth and let rise in pans until they have once again doubled in bulk.

Preheat oven to 350°F. Bake for 45-50 minutes until golden brown. Remove from pans and place on cooling rack. If you prefer a soft crust, brush a small amount of oil along top.

solstice parachute ginger bread

Preheat oven to 350°F.

In a mixing bowl, combine the flour, baking powder, baking soda, ginger powder, cinnamon and salt substitute or sea salt.

In a measuring cup, beat together the molasses, oil, coconut sugar and coconut milk. Add to dry ingredients.

Batter should be light and spill into a 8x8-inch pan like one big cookie dough. Sprinkle the sesame seeds on top.

Bake for 40 minutes. Cool before serving with good quality vegan butter.

lassy bread anyone

Makes 2 loaves

1 tsp raw organic sugar

¾ cup warm water

2 tbsp dry active yeast

2½ cups unsweetened coconut milk

¼ cup sunflower oil

1 tbsp sea salt

½ cup unsulfured molasses

6-7 cups light flour

2 tsp cinnamon

1 tsp mace

1 tsp cloves

2 cups raisins (soaked in 1 cup warm water)

In a measuring cup, dissolve yeast in lukewarm water to which 1 tsp raw sugar has been added. Leave undisturbed for 10-15 minutes until yeast is bubbly.

Meanwhile, in a saucepan, warm the coconut milk, but do not boil. Turn off heat and add oil, sea salt, and molasses. Next, add yeast mixture.

In a large bowl, mix 3 cups of flour with the cinnamon, mace, and cloves. Add the liquid mixture to the flour mixture. Beat all together with wooden spoon for 2-3 minutes. Continue adding flour until a moist soft dough is formed, up to 3 more cups. Drain raisins and add to dough. Retain raisin water.

Place the dough on a floured table or board and knead for 10 minutes until dough becomes smooth and elastic (add more flour if dough is sticky). Clean and lightly oil the mixing bowl.

Return dough to the bowl, the round mound up. Cover with a cloth. Set in a warm place until double in bulk, about 2 hours.

Divide dough in half and shape to form 2 loaves. As you knead with your hands, make the surface smooth and elastic (add a few sprinkles of flour if dough is sticky).

Place in 2 oiled 5x9-inch loaf pans. Cover again with a cloth and allow to rise again until double (about 1 hour).

Preheat oven to 350°F and bake for 50 minutes, until loaves are brown and sound hollow when tapped. Remove from oven and turn onto a cooling rack. Brush tops with coconut oil while hot.

Allow to cool, if you can wait, before cutting.

Connie's banana bread (revised for a vegan gluten-free diet)

1 cup coconut milk

¼ cup light oil

½ cup organic coconut sugar

1 tsp orange zest

1 tsp pure vanilla or almond extract

1 tbsp egg replacer mixed with ¼ cup water

2 cups gluten-free flour mixture

1 tsp baking powder

1 tsp baking soda

pinch sea salt

3 ripe (speckled) organic bananas

Preheat oven to 350°F.

Add coconut milk, light oil, coconut sugar, orange zest, vanilla or almond extract, and prepared egg replacer to a food processor and blend for just one minute.

Combine the gluten-free flour mixture, baking powder, baking soda, and sea salt. Then add the flour mixture to the liquid ingredients and blend for another minute.

In a bowl, mash the bananas then add them by hand to the blended mixture. Do not over stir.

Pour into oiled bread pan or use parchment paper on bottom of loaf pan. Bake for 50 minutes.

Let stand a few minutes and then remove from bread pan to a cooling rack.

sour dough bread starter

Sour Dough is one of the wonders created in your kitchen that can be used again and again to provide a great deal of nutrition. A homemade yeast rises the bread and adds a unique flavour to every loaf. In fact, even people who suffer from digestive problems or who have sensitive stomachs can digest sour dough as the lectins are destroyed in the fermentation process. Since sour dough is a living organism, you have to keep it alive to serve you well for months, even years. Here's how. The next time you make bread, reserve 2 cups of dough for this starter.

sour dough starter

2 cups of bread dough

1 cup of water (approx.)

1 cup flour

1 cup warm water

Knead two cups of bread dough and then cover it with a cloth and allow to rise until it doubles in bulk.

In a ceramic bowl, cover dough with water (about 1 cup) and stir in. Put saran wrap or a loose lid over the top of the bowl. Refrigerate until ready to use. Begin to use the starter at least a week after you put it in the fridge.

When you are ready to make Sour Dough Bread, retain half of the sour dough starter, add 1 cup of flour and 1 cup of warm water to the original starter and stir. It will be much like a pancake batter but even more stringy. Let sit at room temperature for 1 hour, covered with saran wrap. Return to refrigerator and it will be ready to use again and again.

sour dough bread

1 cup sour dough bread starter

2 cups warm water

2 tsp sea salt

1 tbsp coconut sugar

⅔ cup light oil, sunflower or avocado

2 cups flour, your choice

Stir the sour dough bread starter, warm water, salt, sugar and oil together and cover. Let sit at room temperature in a ceramic bowl for at least 6 hours.

Add 1 cup flour with a wooden spoon. Knead in another cup to prevent dough from sticking to the bowl. Oil the top of the dough, cover bowl with saran wrap, and let sit overnight.

In the morning, shape loaves as desired. Depending on their size, you will have 2 or 3 loaves.

Place on a baking sheet with parchment paper, leaving 4-6 inches between loaves. Spread a little oil over top of the loaves. Cover again with saran wrap. The oil on the loaves will prevent the dough from sticking to the saran wrap when it rises. Let sit for another 4-6 hours.

Preheat oven to 375°F. Before baking, score loaves with a sharp knife to add your signature to the loaf.

Bake for 40 minutes or until golden brown.

pita bread

1 tsp coconut sugar

1 cup warm water

1½ tsp baker's yeast

1 tsp sea salt

3 cups flour

1½ tbsp extra virgin olive oil

In a small bowl, mix 1 tsp of coconut sugar into the warm water. Sprinkle the baker's yeast over the water and allow to dissolve and rise for ten minutes.

In a large bowl, mix the sea salt and flour.

Mix flour, yeast, and oil thoroughly with a wooden spoon. Knead for 10 minutes, adding a sprinkling of flour as you knead to prevent dough from sticking to bowl. Shape into round ball.

Oil bowl, cover with a fresh cloth, and let rise for 90 minutes in a warm place.

Punch dough and knead again for 5 minutes. On a floured board, divide into 6 equal parts. Cover with your fresh tea towel and let stand for 15 minute.

Roll to ¼-inch thickness. Place on un-oiled baking tray or baking stone.

Preheat oven to 475°F. Bake on lowest possible oven rack for 5 minutes or until puffed and brown. Serve fresh.

Wrap the freshly baked breads in a towel and place in a brown paper bag. This serves to maintain their thin pockets as they deflate, preventing them from crumbling into crackers. If they do crumble to crackers, enjoy with soup!

figgy duff

2 cups sifted flour

1 tsp baking soda

1 tsp ginger

1 tsp allspice

1 tsp cinnamon

½ tsp sea salt

½ cup molasses

¼ cup oil or melted vegan butter

2 tbsp hot water

1 tbsp egg replacer dissolved in ¼ cup water

1 cup raisins

MOLASSES CODY

1 cup molasses

¼ cup water

¼ cup vegan butter

1 tbsp lemon juice

A revised recipe I originally received from my mother, Florence White. Figgy Duff is a traditional Newfoundland raisin pudding boiled in a dye-free cloth bag and served steaming hot. Figgy refers to the raisins and duff *to the dough mixture (*dough *was sometimes pronounced* duff *in British dialect).*

In a mixing bowl, combine the sifted flour, baking soda, ginger, allspice, cinnamon, and sea salt.

In a measuring cup, combine molasses, oil or melted vegan butter, hot water, and dissolved egg replacer.

Add the wet mixture to the dry mixture and then fold in the raisins.

Spoon the dough into a pudding bag or mold. Place mold in steamer or large pot and add boiling water to pot. Immerse the pudding into the pot, add enough water halfway up sides of pudding mold. Cover and steam for 2 hours or until firm to touch.

If you are using a cloth pudding bag, place bag in enough boiling water to cover the bag. When cooked, remove from water, immediately open the bag, and release pudding onto a serving dish.

Serve with Molasses Cody (my mother's word for coating or sauce for pudding).

TO MAKE THE MOLASSES CODY

Combine all ingredients in a saucepan, bring to a boil, and then simmer for 10 minutes. Serve hot poured over pudding.

dough balls anyone

2 cups flour

5 tsp baking powder

¼ tsp sea salt

½ cup sunflower oil

1 cup cold water (approx.)

A revised traditional recipe from my sister, Angela Slaney. Most often served with stew or soup.

Mix together the flour, baking powder, and sea salt. Then cut in the sunflower oil. Add enough cold water to form a dough.

Using a soup spoon, drop individual spoonfuls into bubbling soup. Cover and let steam-cook for 15 minutes.

Remove from soup and arrange on a platter. Separate with two forks so they will not go soggy.

blueberry dumplings
(variation as a dessert)

2½ cups flour

4½ tsp baking powder

1 tsp sea salt

1 tbsp vegetable oil

1 cup coconut milk

Combine the flour, baking powder, salt, and vegetable oil in a mixing bowl and stir in coconut milk until moist.

Shape dough into small 2-inch balls. Drop into hot and bubbling blueberry sauce. Cover pot tightly and do not lift cover for 15 minutes. Yum!

Serve on their own or with coconut or soy cream.

[cornmeal bread]

cornmeal buns or bread

1 cup organic cornmeal

1 cup coconut and quinoa flour combination

2 tsp baking powder

1 tsp baking soda

1 tsp sea salt

1 tbsp organic coconut sugar

1 cup coconut milk

¼ cup light oil

1 tbsp flax meal mixed with ½ cup water

Preheat oven to 350°F.

In a mixing bowl, sift together the cornmeal, coconut and quinoa flour combination, baking powder, baking soda, sea salt, and organic coconut sugar. Set aside.

Combine the coconut milk, light oil, and flax meal mixed with water and then add to the flour mixture.

Spoon into muffin tins or a loaf pan.

Bake for 20 minutes. If you use a loaf pan, bake for 30 minutes.

tofu herb rolls

1 tbsp baker's yeast

1½ cup warm water

1 tbsp organic coconut sugar

3 cups flour

1 tsp sea salt

½ tsp dill weed

½ tsp chives

1 onion, minced

2 cloves garlic, minced

16 oz soft tofu, drained and mashed

½ cup flour, for kneading

2 tbsp vegan butter

½ cup sesame seeds

Revised from a recipe by Sheila Moore.

Sprinkle baker's yeast in a small bowl and add warm water and coconut sugar. Let rise for 15 minutes until yeast is light and foamy.

Add 3 cups of flour to a mixing bowl and then add the risen yeast and stir. Add sea salt, dill, chives, onion, and garlic. Drain and mash the tofu and stir into dough. Gradually add a sprinkling of flour to sides of bowl. Knead dough for 5 minutes and form into a ball. Punch down and let rest for 20 minutes.

Form into bun-size balls and sprinkle on sesame seeds. Place on oiled baking sheet and lightly flatten with a fork. The balls should barely touch each other. Let rise again until double in bulk.

Preheat oven to 375°F and bake for 20 minutes. Cool on a wire rack.

Quidi Vidi Road soup biscuits

Makes 12 fluffy biscuits to serve with stew or soup

1½ cups spelt flour

½ cup organic corn flour

1 tsp dehydrated vegetable seasoning

1 tbsp no alum baking powder

4 tbsp organic sugar

½ cup avocado oil

½ cup coconut milk

Preheat oven to 350°F.

Combine spelt flour, corn flour, dehydrated vegetable seasoning, and baking powder.

Cut in organic sugar and avocado oil. Add enough coconut milk and stir to make stiff consistency.

Spoon onto parchment paper or oiled cookie sheet and gently flatten with a wet fork. Bake for 20 minutes.

CROSSES

1 tbsp organic white flour

4 tbsp organic sugar

4 tbsp water (or enough to make a paste)

GLAZE

4 tbsp organic white sugar

2 tbsp hot water

BUNS

2½ tsp dry active quick baking yeast

1 cup warm water

1 tsp organic sugar

3½ + ¾ cups all-purpose flour

1 tsp cinnamon

1 tsp ground nutmeg

¼ tsp allspice

1 tsp pink salt

¼ cup organic sugar

1 tbsp egg replacer dissolved in ¼ cup spring water

⅓ cup coconut oil or vegan butter

1 cup unsweetened coconut milk

1½ cups organic raisins

zest of 1 lemon

zest of 1 orange

Fanny's hot cross buns

It wouldn't be spring without spiced hot-cross buns baking in the oven. Traditionally, they are served on Good Friday. Grandma Fanny would save a piece of the dough, cover it with hot water, and keep it in a cool place to use a bit at a time as a poultice to draw out a splinter or cover a garden wound. These are best made in the early morning light.

TO MAKE THE CROSSES

In a small mixing bowl, add the organic white flour. Combine the sugar and water to form a paste and then mix with the flour. Set aside.

TO MAKE THE GLAZE

Mix the organic white sugar in the hot water. Set aside.

TO MAKE THE BUNS

In a measuring cup, dissolve the baking yeast in the warm water with 1 tsp of organic sugar. Set aside and allow yeast to dissolve and rise for 15 minutes until foamy.

In a large bowl, add 3½ cups flour, cinnamon, nutmeg, allspice, salt, and sugar.

In a second bowl or measuring cup, add the dissolved egg replacer and stir in coconut oil and coconut milk. Add the risen yeast to the liquid ingredients and stir to mix.

Pour liquid mixture into the dry ingredients. Continue to mix until all flour has been combined. It will be sticky at this point. Add up to an additional ¾ cup of flour, a little at a time. Work the dough into a ball with a wooden spoon. Add raisins and the lemon and orange zest. Cover bowl with a clean tea towel and allow to rise in a warm area for about 2 hours.

CONTINUES ▶

After the dough has doubled in bulk, dust a clean, dry work surface with flour and turn dough onto it, making sure nothing is left in the bowl. Do not tear the dough. You will need to add a few sprinkles of flour to the surface of the dough or it will stick to your hands. Dust top of dough with flour and begin to shape the dough, making it round. Cut into 12 even pieces. Shape each piece into round balls by pulling the dough under your hands to make it tight. Place buns on a lightly floured board or lined baking sheet, leaving enough space around each bun for them to expand. Cover with the same tea towel and allow to rise for 30 more minutes.

Preheat oven to 400°F. Remove cloth from buns, and dip kitchen scissors into a glass of warm water and gently cut a deep cross into the centre of each bun. Using a piping bag, spread a thin layer of the crosses mixture into each bun cross. Bake for 12-15 minutes or until golden brown.

Remove from oven and immediately brush glaze over each bun. Do not skimp on the glaze. Transfer to a cooling rack. Serve warm with your favourite vegan buttery spread.

> **I SOMETIMES** broil the buns for 1 minute, but do not leave unattended for a second or you run the risk of burning your precious buns.

Figgie Lizzie tea buns

1 cup coconut milk

2 tbsp egg replacer mixed with ¼ cup water

½ cup vegan butter

4 cups light flour

2 tbsp baking powder

1 tsp pink Himalayan salt

½ cup raw organic sugar

1½ cups organic raisins (soaked and drained)

I learnt this recipe from my mother, Florence, who learnt it from her mother, Mabel Hall, who came to Newfoundland from Failsworth, England. During my Ottawa school days and through my roommate, Kathleen Small, this recipe ended up on the menu of an international ambassador's conference in Beijing, China, and was so enjoyed that several ambassadors asked to have the recipe for their kitchen tea menu. Thus they are enjoyed around the world. Mother loved to hear that story.

Preheat oven to 375°F.

In a large measuring cup, whisk together the coconut milk and dissolved egg replacer.

In mixing bowl, stir together flour, baking powder, pink salt, and sugar. Cut in vegan butter with a pastry cutter.

Add wet mixture to flour mixture. Stir enough to combine all ingredients and add the raisins last.

Put dough on a floured table or board and fold dough several times. Let rest for 10 minutes.

Roll dough lightly to 1-inch thickness. Cut in 2-inch diameter circles with a small glass or circular cookie cutter. Place on an oiled cookie sheet, almost joining buns to each other. Bake for 20 minutes.

Break one open to test for a perfectly baked bun. It should be dry throughout. Buns may be turned onto a cloth and separated from each other.

Delicious with lecithin spread or vegan butter (for old times' sake). Serve warm with tea. My favourite hot drink is chai tea, brewed with coconut milk. Treat yourself now.

Makes 12 muffins

2 cups spelt flour (or your choice of flour)

½ cup almond flour

½ cup coconut flour

3 tsp aluminum-free baking powder

½ tsp pink Himalayan salt

½ cup coconut sugar

2 tbsp egg replacer dissolved in ¼ cup water

½ cup melted coconut oil

1 tbsp flax meal

2 cups almond or coconut milk

1 tsp pure vanilla

1 cup fresh or frozen blueberries

not so old-fashioned coconut blueberry muffins

Preheat oven to 375°F.

In a mixing bowl, combine the spelt flour, almond flour, coconut flour, baking powder, pink Himalayan salt, and coconut sugar.

In a measuring cup, whisk the dissolved egg replacer, melted coconut oil, flax meal, almond or coconut milk, and vanilla.

Stir liquid ingredients into the bowl with dry ingredients until all flour is well combined, about 2 minutes. Fold blueberries into batter.

Fill oiled muffin cups almost full. Bake for 25 minutes.

Serve with almond butter and warm Grandmother Hall's Blueberry Jam.

Grandmother Hall's blueberry jam

Simmer 2 cups of blueberries in ¼ cup of spring water. Bring to boil and simmer while muffins are baking. After ten minutes, stir in ½ cup coconut sugar.

Grandmother Hall was a superb jam maker who honed her skills while working in a jam factory in her native Manchester, England.

HINT: For thicker jam, dissolve 1 tbsp arrowroot flour in 1 tbsp water and stir into jam.

apple streusel berry muffins

Created during a rainy Victoria Day weekend, this recipe makes 12 tasty muffins.

TOPPING

¼ cup organic coconut sugar

1 tbsp organic coconut flour

1 tbsp melted coconut oil or vegan buttery spread

½ tsp ground cinnamon

MUFFINS

2 cups organic spelt flour

½ cup organic coconut sugar

½ cup quinoa flakes

½ tsp pink Himalayan salt

2 tbsp aluminum-free baking powder

½ tsp baking soda

2 tbsp egg replacer dissolved in ¼ cup spring water

¼ cup sunflower oil

1 cup coconut milk

1 small organic apple, finely diced

TO MAKE THE TOPPING
In a small mixing bowl, mix all ingredients into a crumble. Set aside.

TO MAKE THE MUFFINS
Preheat oven to 375°F.

In a mixing bowl, combine the spelt flour, coconut sugar, quinoa flakes, salt, baking powder, and baking soda.

In a 4-cup measuring bowl, hand mix the dissolved egg replacer, sunflower oil, and coconut milk and then combine with dry ingredients. Hand stir until moist, but do not overmix.

Cut in the finely diced organic apple. Stir only enough to mix.

Add up to ½ cup more coconut milk if mixture is too thick. You should be able to easily spoon into the muffin cups. Fill muffin cups ¾ full and sprinkle with topping.

Bake for 25 minutes. Let cool 5 minutes before placing on a cooling rack. Serve warm with blueberry jam.

[apple streusel berry muffins]

lightweight quinoa muffins

Makes 12 high-fibre muffins

1 cup quinoa flakes

2 cups spelt flour (or any light flour)

1 tbsp aluminum-free baking powder

½ tsp allspice

½ tsp cloves

½ cup coconut sugar

1 tbsp egg replacer dissolved in ¼ cup water

2 tbsp sunflower oil

1 cup coconut or any nut milk

1 tsp pure vanilla

½ cup molasses

½ cup chopped walnuts

½ cup pitted dates, chopped small

Preheat oven to 375°F.

In a mixing bowl, combine quinoa flakes, spelt flour, baking powder, allspice, cloves, and coconut sugar.

In a measuring cup, combine the dissolved egg replacer, sunflower oil, coconut milk, vanilla, and molasses.

Combine wet mixture with dry ingredients. Fold in chopped walnuts and dates, just enough to combine with batter. Add up to ½ cup coconut milk if batter is too stiff or dry.

Spoon into oiled muffin tins, and bake for 25 minutes.

HINT: When making muffins, if there is not enough batter to fill the muffin cups, half fill the empty ones with water. This keeps the temperature even while baking.

Margaret Atwood wheat germ muffins
(revised and edited)

Makes 12 muffins

1 cup organic sugar

1 tbsp egg replacer dissolved in ¼ cup water

⅓ cup sunflower oil

2 cups almond milk

1 tsp pure vanilla

1 apple, diced

2 cups spelt flour

1 tsp baking soda

2 tsp baking powder

½ tsp sea salt

2 cups wheat germ or 1 cup quinoa flakes

1 cup partridge berries (fresh or frozen)

1 cup diced apple

I originally found Margaret Atwood Wheat Germ Muffins in the light-hearted Canadian Literature Foodbook. *Later, I revised and edited the ingredients to suit my dietary regime. Joan Clarke presented Atwood with a copy of my* Eldamar Cookbook, *which included this recipe, when she visited St. John's in the late 1990s. Makes a dozen muffins and one tester.*

Preheat oven to 375°F.

Whip together by hand, or in food processor, the organic sugar, dissolved egg replacer, sunflower oil, almond milk, and vanilla. Set aside.

In a mixing bowl, combine the spelt flour, baking soda, baking powder, sea salt, and wheat germ (or quinoa flakes).

Add the dry ingredients to the liquid ingredients. Do not over blend. Then fold in by hand the partridgeberries and diced apple.

Spoon into muffin tins. Bake for 25 minutes.

sweet memory scones

Makes 8 scones

1 cup spelt flour

½ cup almond flour

½ cup quinoa flour

1 tbsp baking powder

¼ tsp sea salt

2 tbsp oil

1 tbsp egg replacer dissolved in ¼ cup water

¼ cup sunflower oil

½ cup organic almond milk

2 tbsp maple syrup

Preheat oven to 375°F.

Sift together the spelt flour, almond flour, quinoa flour, baking powder, and sea salt. Mix 2 tbsp oil into the flour with your fingers until lumpy.

In a separate bowl, whip together the dissolved egg replacer, sunflower oil, almond milk, and maple syrup. Mix into dry ingredients until moist.

Add just enough flour to enable you to roll out dough on a floured cutting board. Divide dough into 2 equal parts, ½-inch thick. Cut into four wedges and divide again to make 8 scones.

Oil a baking pan with a few drops of oil and lightly flour the bottom of the pan. Bake for 20 minutes.

Serve warm with homemade jam.

Makes 12 scones

TOPPING

1 tbsp coconut milk

½ tsp cinnamon

1 tbsp coconut sugar

SCONES

1½ cups flour

½ cup coconut flour

½ cup organic coconut sugar

2 tsp aluminum-free baking powder

½ tsp baking soda

½ tsp Himalayan salt

1 tsp ginger

1 tsp cinnamon

¼ cup melted coconut oil

1 cup coconut milk

1 small organic apple, peeled and grated

1 pear, peeled and grated

½ cup spelt flour

apple pear pie scones

TO MAKE THE TOPPING

Mix all ingredients together. Whisk and brush over top of prepared scones.

TO MAKE THE SCONES

Preheat oven to 400°F.

In a mixing bowl, combine flour, coconut flour, organic coconut sugar, baking powder, baking soda, Himalayan salt, ginger, and cinnamon. Set aside.

In a measuring cup, cream together the melted coconut oil and coconut milk and then cut into dry ingredients.

Stir the grated apple into the mixture just enough to combine all ingredients and then add the grated pear. Fold several times into one round scone, mixing in the spelt flour.

Make a ¼-inch deep pizza cut to braise the large scone and place in round lightly oiled pan. (Option: Divide dough into 12 pieces and place side by side in baking pan.) Brush on the topping.

Bake for 15-20 minutes. Serve warm.

➤ **FOR VERY** Blue Scones, instead of pear, add ½ cup fresh or frozen blueberries.

Doyle's zucchini loaf

½ cup avocado oil

2 tsp egg replacer dissolved in 2 tbsp water

1 tsp pure vanilla

1 cup grated zucchini

1 cup grated organic apple

2 cups all-purpose flour

1 tsp aluminum-free baking powder

1 tsp baking soda

½ tsp pink Himalayan salt

2 tsp cinnamon

½ tsp nutmeg

1 cup raw organic coconut sugar

½ cup chopped organic walnuts (optional)

½ cup organic dark chocolate chips

Preheat oven to 350°F.

In a large measuring cup, hand mix the avocado oil, dissolved egg replacer, and vanilla. Add the grated zucchini and grated apple.

In a mixing bowl, combine flour, baking powder, baking soda, salt, cinnamon, nutmeg, and coconut sugar.

Combine dry ingredients with zucchini mixture and stir until all flour is incorporated into the mix. Lastly, stir in the chopped walnuts (optional) and organic dark chocolate chips (not optional).

Pour into an oiled loaf pan or bread pan and bake for 50 minutes.

HINT: Place a square sheet of parchment paper on bottom and sides of baking dish or sprinkle a pinch of flour on bottom of baking dish to prevent loaf from sticking to pan.

When cooked, the top of the loaf will crack slightly. Remove from heat and let stand in loaf pan 10 minutes before transferring to a cooling rack. Slice. Before serving, add chocolate sauce or homemade coconut ice cream.

Option: Blend the first 12 ingredients in food processor for 3 minutes. Add walnuts and chocolate chips and hand stir into mixture.

special occasion pancakes

1 cup spelt flour

½ cup coconut flour

½ cup organic cornmeal

3 tsp aluminum-free baking powder

1 tbsp coconut sugar

pinch sea salt

1 tbsp avocado oil

1 tbsp egg replacer dissolved in ¼ cup water

2 cups almond milk

In a mixing bowl, combine spelt flour, coconut flour, cornmeal, baking powder, coconut sugar, and sea salt.

In a measuring cup, hand blend the avocado oil, dissolved egg replacer, and almond milk.

Make a canyon hole in centre of flour mixture. Add hand-blended milk mixture into the canyon hole slowly until mixture becomes easy to stir. Lumpy batter works best.

Fry evenly over medium heat. Serve with maple syrup or *la confiture de fraise*.

scorpio sun celebration pancakes

1 cup flour

½ cup organic cornmeal

½ cup coconut flour

½ tsp cinnamon

4 tsp aluminum-free baking powder

½ tsp baking soda

¼ tsp pink Himalayan salt

2 tbsp coconut sugar

1 tbsp flax meal

3 cups coconut or almond milk

2 tbsp egg replacer dissolved in ¼ cup water

3 tbsp light oil

1 additional cup of almond milk (on reserve)

Combine all ingredients, but do not over mix. Batter will thicken so you will need to add up to 1 more cup of coconut or almond milk. Fry evenly over medium heat. Serve with raw almond butter, apricot spread and maple syrup.

yesteryear pancakes for today's diet

1 cup wheat-free flour

½ cup almond flour

½ cup coconut flour

1 tsp cinnamon

½ tsp nutmeg

4 tsp aluminum-free baking powder

2 tbsp coconut sugar

2 tbsp egg replacer dissolved in ¼ cup water

2 tbsp sunflower oil

1 tbsp maple syrup

2 cups coconut milk

1 cup peeled and grated apple

Wisk together the light oil and almond milk.

Measure and mix the light flour, baking powder, coconut sugar, and cinnamon.

Combine the liquid ingredients with the flour mixture. Aim for the consistency of a light pancake batter.

Fry evenly for the treat of your dairy-less pancake days. Serve with Quebec maple syrup.

➥ **VARY THE** recipe by adding ½ cup blueberries or other small berry.

heavenly crepes

1 cup spelt flour or wheat-free flour

2 tbsp egg replacer dissolved in ¼ cup water

1 cup coconut milk

1 tbsp melted coconut oil

½ tsp stevia

Combine all ingredients with a whisk. Batter should be thin enough to pour into pan.

Heat a flat skillet over medium heat. Use cast iron for best results.

Melt 1 tsp coconut oil in the skillet per crepe. Add ½ cup batter to pan, spreading batter evenly over the surface. Cook until bottom of crepe is golden brown. Turn and briefly cook other side.

Remove crepe from pan and spread with almond or sesame butter. Fill crepes with apple sauce. Fold away from you and pour a dollop of Soy Cream (page 25) or coconut yogurt and a dribble of maple syrup on top of the rolled crepe.

magic potion apple pancakes (1986)

1 cup spelt flour

½ cup almond flour

½ cup coconut flour

1 tsp cinnamon

½ tsp nutmeg

4 tsp aluminum-free baking powder

2 tbsp coconut sugar

2 tbsp egg replacer dissolved in ¼ cup water

2 tbsp sunflower oil

1 tbsp maple syrup

2 cups coconut milk

1 cup peeled and grated apple

As children, Anahareo and my nephew, Django, made magic potions while I made these pancakes.

In a mixing bowl, combine spelt flour, almond flour, coconut flour, cinnamon, nutmeg, baking powder, and coconut sugar.

In a large measuring cup, hand blend the dissolved egg replacer, sunflower oil, maple syrup, and coconut milk. Mix the liquid mixture into the dry ingredients. Add the grated apple.

Fry on medium heat until bubbles start to show through. Turn only once and fry other side. Serve warm with tahini spread, raspberry sauce, and pure maple syrup.

ackee savoury crepes

FILLING

1 small onion, diced

8 oz organic soft tofu, mashed

1 cup Jamaican Ackee

½ cup mushrooms, cut small

½ cup chopped organic red bell pepper

1 clove garlic, crushed

1 tsp savoury and thyme combination

1 tsp Bragg Liquid Soy Seasoning or soy sauce

1 tbsp nutritional yeast

1 tsp turmeric

1 tsp pink Himalayan salt

CREPES

1 cup spelt flour or wheat-free flour

2 tbsp egg replacer dissolved in ¼ cup water

1 cup coconut milk

1 tbsp melted coconut oil

½ tsp stevia

TO MAKE THE ACKEE TOFU SCRAMBLER FILLING

Sauté all scrambler ingredients together for 10 minutes. Keep warm on low heat.

TO MAKE THE CREPES

Combine all crepe ingredients.

Heat a flat skillet over medium heat. Use cast iron for best results.

Melt 1 tsp coconut oil in the skillet per crepe. Add ½ cup batter to pan, spreading batter evenly over the surface. Cook until bottom of crepe is golden brown. Turn and briefly cook other side.

Remove crepe from pan. Fill one half of crepe with 4 tbsp of scrambler and roll away from you.

Serve with steamed asparagus or garden salad.

pie crust that works
(with thanks to wax paper)

Makes 1 double pie crust

1½ cups unbleached white
or wheat-free flour

1 cup spelt or rice flour

¼ tsp sea salt

⅓ cup spring water

⅓ cup light oil

Sift flours together with the sea salt. Set aside.

Mix water and oil together. Gradually add liquid to flour to form a workable dough. Use a fork to stir lightly, and form dough into a ball using your hands.

Divide dough into two parts. Roll one ball between wax paper and flip onto pie plate.

Now it's ready for apples, blueberries, or other fruit filling. See From Another Time Apple Pie on page 120.

Cover top with pie crust. Make a design on top of crust with your fork. This allows steam to escape as your filling bubbles and bakes.

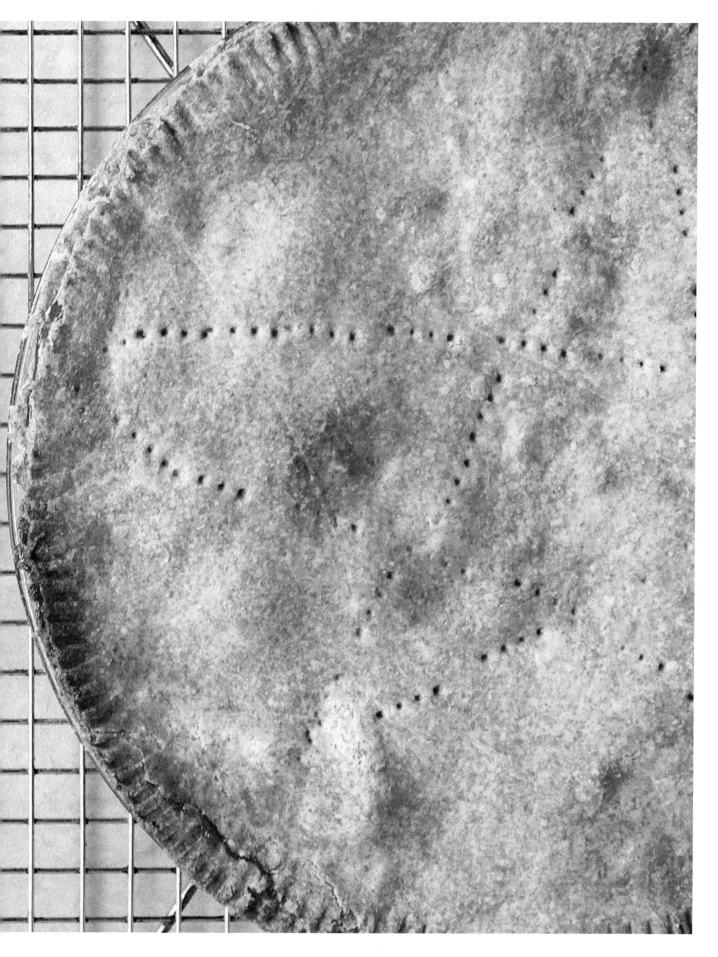

Amelia's raspberry turnovers

2 cups fresh washed raspberries

½ cup coconut sugar

1 tbsp arrowroot flour (sprinkle through berry sugar mixture)

Prepare Pie Crust That Works (page 116).

Preheat oven to 400°F.

For every cup of raspberries, use at least ¼ cup coconut sugar. In a bowl, combine the raspberries and coconut sugar and sprinkle the arrowroot flour through the mixture.

Roll out pastry and cut in 2½-inch squares. Place 2 tbsp of raspberry mixture in the middle of each the square. Fold corner to corner.

Press edges with a fork, and prick surface of dough to allow steam to escape. Bake for 20-25 minutes until raspberries bubble through pastry.

from another time apple pie

4 cups thinly sliced apples

½ cup water

3 tbsp arrowroot flour

2 tsp coriander

1 tsp cinnamon

2 tsp lemon juice

½ cup coconut sugar

¼ tsp sea salt

Preheat oven to 400°F.

In a saucepan, cook apples lightly for 5 minutes in ½ cup water. Drain liquid and retain in a measuring cup.

Add liquid to arrowroot flour and stir with a fork until all lumps are gone. Add this to hot apples to thicken the fruit.

Next add coriander, cinnamon, lemon juice, coconut sugar, and salt. Pour the mixture into your pie crust. Cover with top crust.

Seal edges with a fork and, with the fork, print your favourite design on top of the crust: mine is a star.

Bake for 30 minutes until golden brown.

no tricks pumpkin pie

3 cups fresh pumpkin

¾ cup organic raw sugar

¼ cup Quebec maple syrup

1 tbsp cinnamon

1 tsp ground ginger

¼ tsp nutmeg

¼ tsp cloves

1 cup coconut milk or cream

1 tbsp egg replacer (or organic corn flour) dissolved in 2 tbsp spring water

Clean and cut pumpkin into even slices and remove seeds. Steam, with skin on, until the pumpkin flesh is soft. The skin will be easier to remove once the pumpkin is steamed.

Preheat oven to 400°F.

Blend 3 cups of fresh pumpkin in a food processor until smooth. Strain through a cylinder to remove any excess pulp.

In a mixing bowl, add and mix the fresh pumpkin, sugar, maple syrup, cinnamon, ginger, nutmeg, cloves, coconut milk, and dissolved egg replacer (or corn flour).

Pour into unbaked pie shell and bake for 30 minutes.

[from another time
apple pie]

raspberry tofu cheeseless "cheesecake"

4 cups medium to firm tofu

1½ cups coconut sugar

¼ cup fresh lemon juice

1 tbsp vanilla

pinch sea salt

TOPPING

1 cup raspberries

2 tbsp maple syrup

2 tbsp arrowroot flour

For best results, do not use soft tofu. Medium works best.

Preheat oven to 375°F. Using a springform pan, prepare one 9-inch round graham-cracker pie shell for bottom crust. When possible, to make your life easier, use a cheesecake pan with removable bottom.

Blend all ingredients in a food processor or blender for 3 minutes.

Pour into pie shells and bake for 50 minutes. Pie will slightly crack when done.

Chill for 2 hours and prepare a raspberry sauce for the topping. Once assembled, chill for another two hours.

TO MAKE THE TOPPING

Combine all ingredients in a small saucepan and heat for 1 minute.

coconut almond coffeeless cake

Makes 12 tasty, individual coffeeless cakes

1 cup rice flour or any gluten-free flour

½ cup coconut flour

½ cup almond flour

½ cup organic coconut sugar

2 tsp aluminum-free baking powder

½ tsp pink Himalayan salt

½ cup coconut oil, melted

1 tbsp egg replacer dissolved in ¼ cup water

1 cup coconut milk

½ tsp pure vanilla

SPICE MIX

½ cup coconut sugar

1 tbsp coconut flour

1 tsp cinnamon

1 tbsp carb powder (optional)

Mix together the ingredients for the spice mix and set aside. Only add the carb powder if you'd like a chocolatey effect.

Preheat oven to 400°F.

In a mixing bowl, stir together the flours, coconut sugar, baking powder and salt. Make a well in the centre. Set aside.

Beat coconut oil, and dissolved egg replacer together. Mix in coconut milk and vanilla. Pour into the well in the dry ingredients. Stir until moist.

Spoon batter into oiled muffin tins until each cup is half full. Sprinkle spice mix over top.

Spoon the rest of the batter over top, filling until almost full. Any remaining spice mix can be used on top of the coffeeless cakes.

Bake for 25 minutes.

wild blueberry pie

4 cups fresh blueberries

½ cup organic coconut sugar

½ tsp nutmeg

½ tsp cinnamon

3 tbsp arrowroot flour

1 tbsp lemon juice

2 tbsp vegan butter

Make pastry for 2 pie crusts. Roll out half the pastry and use it to line a pie plate. Edges of the pastry should hang over the rim of the pie plate. Reserve second half for top.

Preheat oven to 400°F.

Toss blueberries with ¼ cup coconut sugar, nutmeg, cinnamon, arrowroot, and lemon juice. Pour into pie shell and mound berries slightly in the middle. Spread remaining coconut sugar over berries. Dot with vegan butter.

Roll out rest of pastry and carefully cover berry filling. Fold edge of bottom crust over edge of top crust and press together with a fork. Design the top crust using a fork, making holes to allow steam to escape. You can also make lattice strips for top.

Bake 30 minutes or until crust is golden brown and berries bubble through pastry.

main dishes

with trimmings

Naeme's tofu burgers

16 oz firm organic tofu

1 medium onion, minced fine

4 tbsp shredded carrot

1 tbsp minced red pepper

4 small mushrooms, chopped

1 tbsp thyme, crumbled fine

1 tbsp basil, crumbled fine

2 tbsp nutritional yeast

1 tbsp organic vegetable seasoning

2 tbsp chickpea flour

2 tbsp avocado oil

oil for frying

8-10 pita breads

shredded lettuce, enough for 8-10 servings

8-10 dill pickles

Mix first 11 ingredients. This is fairly crumbly. A burger patty maker would help in this next step, or use your hands and form into tofu burgers, using a little more chickpea flour to hold burgers together.

Fry at medium heat until golden on each side.

Heat pita breads in moderate oven only long enough to soften them, about one minute.

Cut off top of pita bread, and stuff pita with the tofu burger, lettuce, pickles, and your favourite burger dressings.

HINT: The secret to this recipe is to freeze your tofu for at least 2 hours. Then thaw tofu about 1 hour. When thawed, squeeze excess water through a cloth.

quinoa veggie burgers

1 cup quinoa, cooked

1 cup pea flour and quinoa flour combination

½ cup finely chopped onion

½ cup ground sunflower seeds

1 tsp parsley

1 tsp thyme

2 cloves garlic, minced

1 tbsp or 1 cube organic vegetable bouillon

1 tsp pink Himalayan salt

2 tbsp nutritional yeast

2 tbsp wheat-free soy sauce

2 tbsp organic cornmeal

2 tbsp avocado oil

My personal fave way to eat these burgers is to spread Dijon mustard and organic ketchup on one side of a warm burger bun and vegenaise on the other side. Then add the veggie burger topped with sliced tomato, dill pickle, and a slice of vegan cheese. If you prefer melted cheese, put the slice of vegan cheese on the burger while it is still in the pan. Once assembled on your burger bun, hold together with pea sprouts or lettuce leaves.

Cook 1 cup quinoa in 1½ cups hot water, simmering on low heat for 20 minutes. Once cooked, place quinoa in a stainless-steel bowl.

Add the pea flour and quinoa flour combination, onion, ground sunflower seeds, parsley, thyme, garlic, vegetable bouillon, salt, nutritional yeast, and wheat-free soy sauce. Mix all ingredients together then firm into 2-inch patties and sprinkle with cornmeal.

Fry on both sides in avocado oil. Serve with garden peas and No Fuss Chips (page 173) on the side.

10 large pink potatoes

½ cup almond milk

¼ cup olive oil

2 tsp pink Himalayan salt

1 tsp cracked black pepper

2 tbsp avocado oil

1 large onion, diced

½ cup diced organic green pepper

2 stalks celery, diced

2 cloves garlic, minced

¼ tsp thyme

¼ tsp savoury

¼ tsp basil

¼ tsp oregano

2 cups medium to soft organic tofu, mashed

2 tbsp Bragg Liquid Soy Seasoning

3 corn on the cob

sheppardless pie

Preheat oven to 350°F.

Scrub, cut, and steam the potatoes for about 20 minutes. Mash steamed potatoes, adding a little almond milk, 1 tsp pink Himalayan salt, olive oil and black pepper.

Sauté the avocado oil, onion, green pepper, celery, garlic, and 1 tsp salt for 3 minutes.

Then add thyme, savoury, basil, oregano, mashed tofu, and soy seasoning. Set aside when nicely brown.

Steam the corn for 5 minutes. Allow to cool and then slice corn from cob.

Oil a large casserole dish and spread the sautéed tofu along the bottom. Next, sprinkle corn over the tofu. Top with mashed potatoes, and bake for 20 minutes.

Serve with fresh steamed broccoli, local carrots, and Pagan Vegan Gravy (page 171).

3 cups organic spinach

3 tbsp avocado oil

1 cup diced onion

2 cloves garlic, minced

2 medium sweet potato, peeled and chopped

1 tsp pink Himalayan salt

1 tsp cumin

1 cup grated carrot

½ cup nutritional yeast

1 tbsp lemon juice

1 tsp organic vegetable seasoning

4 medium tomato, cut

10 fresh corn tortillas

SAUCE

1 tbsp avocado oil

1 tbsp organic vegetable bouillon

1 cup unsweetened coconut milk

1 cup coconut cream

½ cup diced chilies

1 tbsp pea flour, mixed with

2 tbsp spring water

spinach enchiladas

Wash, drain, and chop spinach. Set aside.

Heat oil in a large cast-iron pot, sauté onion, garlic, and sweet potato until tender.

Add salt, cumin, carrot, yeast, lemon juice, and vegetable seasoning and continue cooking over medium heat, stirring often.

Add tomato and continue to cook for two more minutes. Add spinach last.

Brush each tortilla with avocado oil and heat them individually in a frying pan for a minute. Spoon mixture into each tortilla, fold and roll.

Preheat oven to 350°F.

Oil a large casserole pot and arrange enchiladas in it, folded end facing down.

Mix all the sauce ingredients together and pour over enchiladas until they are covered.

Sprinkle vegan shredded cheese over rolled enchiladas. Cover and bake for 15 minutes.

Uncover for browning and bake another 5 minutes.

quick summer's meal for three

1 medium butternut squash

2 tbsp vegan butter spread
or olive oil

pinch fresh black pepper to taste

pinch pink Himalayan salt

8 slices of organic tofu

¼ cup soy sauce

juice of 1 lemon

pinch thyme

Preheat oven to 400°F and bake the butternut squash for 45 minutes. It's ready when a fork can be easily inserted through the squash. Remove from oven and cut in half. Remove seeds and place cooked pulp in a bowl. Mash, adding the vegan butter (or olive oil). Season with fresh black pepper and pink Himalayan salt.

Marinate the tofu in soy sauce for 10 minutes. Cover tofu in Tofu Coating (page 172). Squeeze the lemon juice over tofu and a sprinkling of thyme. Sauté for 2 minutes on each side.

➤ THIS RECIPE works really well with Baked Brown Rice (page 146) and steamed Swiss chard.

spanakopita alive and well

6 sheets phyllo pastry

1 cup diced onion

2 cups medium to firm tofu, mashed

1 tbsp vegetable bouillon

1 tsp pink Himalayan salt

1 lb chopped spinach

1 cup Nutritional Yeast Sauce or grated vegan cheese

Preheat oven to 375°F.

Sauté the onion, mashed tofu, vegetable bouillon, salt, and spinach for 10 minutes.

This is a 6-layer dish, so start by spreading 1 sheet of pastry in a 9x13-inch casserole dish. Brush with melted vegan spread. Spoon some sauté mixture over the phyllo. Repeat until the casserole dish is full.

Sprinkle 1 cup Nutritional Yeast Sauce (page 171) on top or grated vegan cheese. Bake for 40 minutes until golden brown.

tempeh casserole

2 tbsp coconut oil

2 cups diced onion

2 cloves garlic, minced

1 cup tempeh

2 medium carrots, julienned

1 stalk celery, thinly julienned

1 small green pepper, thinly sliced

4 ripe tomatoes, quartered

1 tbsp molasses

2 cups chopped organic spinach

1 tsp basil

2 tsp thyme

1 tbsp organic vegetable bouillon cube

1 tsp pink Himalayan salt

1 tsp unsalted Dijon mustard

1 tbsp lemon juice

Preheat oven to 350°F.

Melt the coconut oil in a cast-iron pot and then sauté the onion, garlic, tempeh, carrots, celery, and green pepper. Simmer at medium heat for 10 minutes stirring occasionally.

Hand mix all of the remaining ingredients and add to the sautéed ingredients.

If you use a cast-iron pan, place pan in the oven or pour the mixture into a casserole dish. Bake for 15 minutes.

> ↪ THIS RECIPE is even better when served with baked butternut squash. Preheat the oven to 350°F, and bake for 45 minutes. When fork tender, remove from oven. Cut in half, remove seeds and skin. Mash squash and season lightly with olive oil, salt, and cayenne pepper.

the tacky taco

1 medium onion, chopped

1 medium organic tomato, chopped

6 leaves lettuce, torn into small pieces

1 cup salsa

1 cup shredded vegan cheese

2 cups cooked and mashed organic kidney beans

2 tbsp avocado oil

1 tsp ground chili

1 tbsp chili pepper

1 tsp mineral salt

½ tsp fresh cracked black pepper

6 taco shells

Set aside the onion, tomato, lettuce, salsa, and vegan cheese in individual bowls.

Preheat oven to 350°F.

On medium heat, fry the mashed kidney beans in the avocado oil with the ground chili, chili pepper, mineral salt, and pepper.

Spoon into taco shells. Sprinkle grated vegan cheese over shells or Nutritional Yeast Sauce (page 171). Bake for 15 minutes.

Spoon salsa (page 41) and chopped veggies over the top before serving.

festive barbecue gluten

6 cups unbleached white flour

2 cups whole wheat

2 cups gluten flour

3 cups cold water

½ cup nutritional yeast flakes

½ cup organic peanut butter

1 tbsp paprika

1 tsp pink Himalayan salt

1 medium onion, chopped

½ cup vegetable oil

SAUCE

¼ cup avocado oil

1 large onion, diced

2 cloves garlic, minced

6 cups tomato sauce

½ cup water

4 tbsp organic molasses

½ cup prepared mustard

1 tbsp Bragg Liquid Soy Seasoning

1 tsp allspice

2 tsp cayenne

2 tbsp parsley flakes

¼ cup fresh lemon juice

This unusual and tasty dish is derived from the gluten rib recipe found in Louise Hagler's The Farm Vegetarian Cookbook, *originally published in 1975. It is a labour-intensive recipe, usually undertaken by Beni once a year during the festive season. Definitely not for gluten-sensitive stomachs.*

Start by making the pot of gluten. If you would prefer a more tender gluten, omit the whole wheat and replace it with 2 more cups of gluten flour.

Combine the flours and add the cold water to make a stiff dough. Knead for 15 minutes until the dough feels expansive and flexible. Place in a large stainless-steel bowl and cover with cold water. Let soak for at least 2 hours. Then knead the dough under *cold* water, discarding the water as it turns milky. This removes the starch from the flour, and what remains is the gluten.

Keep the dough together. It will break apart somewhat, but if it begins to fall apart completely you're in trouble! You can still use the gluten, but it will be in small pieces.

Change the water as it fills with white starch, and stop kneading when water has only a slightly starchy appearance. Reserve this gluten (about 8 cups).

Preheat oven to 350°F.

Combine the yeast flakes, peanut butter, paprika, and salt in a bowl and set aside.

Drain off any excess water from the gluten and then knead the peanut-butter mixture into the gluten.

Sauté the onion in the vegetable oil. Then pour hot onions and oil over the gluten. Mix with a wooden spoon and knead the seasoned gluten with your hands. As the oil breaks the gluten down, it will get a little stringy. Tear off chunks of the

CONTINUES ▶

gluten (3x5-inch pieces) and place in a large, well-oiled baking pan. Bake for 50 minutes. Gluten should be crispy and brown on the bottom.

While gluten is baking, prepare the sauce. In a large saucepan, combine all of the ingredients except for the lemon juice. Bring sauce to a boil and then reduce heat to low. Cover and simmer for 20 minutes, stirring occasionally.

When sauce is ready, add the fresh lemon juice.

Remove gluten from the oven and pour sauce over the entire pan. Don't spare the sauce, but reserve at least 1 cup to pour over gluten before serving.

Return to oven and bake for 10 minutes longer.

choux-fleur au gratin (Quebec style)

1 medium cauliflower

1 cup diced organic medium to firm tofu

2 tbsp wheat-free soy sauce or coconut sauce substitute

3 tbsp avocado oil

2 medium onions, diced

1 clove garlic, minced

1 cup coconut milk

3 tbsp yellow pea flour

1 tsp basil

1 tsp parsley

1 tbsp vegetable bouillon

1 cup rice bread croutons (optional)

1 cup grated vegan cheese

Preheat oven to 350°F.

Steam the cauliflower for 5 minutes (retain water). Marinate diced tofu in wheat-free soy sauce, enough to cover tofu. Set aside.

To prepare the sauce, heat oil in a large frying pan and add diced onions and garlic. Fry on medium heat until onions are golden (not brown). Then add flour until all the oil is absorbed. While stirring, add the leftover steaming water used for the cauliflower. Add coconut milk a little at a time to prevent the formation of lumps in the sauce. Cook on medium heat until thick, stirring often. Set the sauce aside.

In a separate frying pan, sauté the marinated tofu.

Place the whole steamed cauliflower in a round casserole dish and top with sautéed tofu. Pour sauce over top of casserole.

Sprinkle croutons on top and spread vegan cheese over top of casserole. Bake for 20 minutes and then broil for 1 minute to brown the top. Do not leave unattended while broiling.

Bon appétit!

veggie pâté à Lorraine

2 cups flour (brown rice, pea, or millet)

½ cup coconut flour

1½ cups sunflower seeds (or 1 cup sunflower and ½ cup sesame seeds)

1 tbsp thyme

1 tbsp basil (or 1 heaping tbsp of fresh pesto)

1 tbsp oregano

2 tbsp savoury

1 tsp sea salt

2 cups nutritional yeast flakes

¼ cup lemon juice

¼ cup wheat-free soy sauce

1 cup avocado oil or other light oil

6 medium onions, quartered

5 large potatoes, quartered

2 cups water

Lorraine Desjardins shared a version of this recipe with me when I had the good fortune of sharing my home with her for almost a year. She revised the original recipe from her father's French pâté, which I have in turn revised again. This dish is a real party favourite. Please do not freeze the pâté as it alters the delicate flavour.

Preheat oven to 350°F.

In a food processor, blend the flour, sunflower seeds, thyme, basil, oregano, savoury, and sea salt for 2 minutes. Pour into a large stainless-steel bowl and stir in the nutritional yeast flakes (do not use brewer's yeast). Set this dry mixture aside.

Add the lemon juice, soy sauce, avocado oil, onions, and potatoes to your food processor and blend until smooth. Depending on the size of your food processor, you may need to divide these ingredients and blend them in more than one batch.

Combine wet ingredients with the dry mixture and hand mix until all ingredients are well combined.

Boil 2 cups of water and allow it to cool slightly before adding it to the mixture. Mix with a wooden spoon until all ingredients are once again well combined.

Pour into one lightly oiled 9x12-inch pan and one 5x8-inch pan. Pâté should be about 1 inch high. Bake for 50 minutes. Cool for ten minutes before cutting.

Serve hot as a main dish or spread on crackers with Dijon mustard and a hint of pesto.

eggplant comes around

2 small or 1 large eggplant

2 + 1 tbsp Bragg Liquid Soy Seasoning

1 cup medium to firm tofu

1 cup water

3 cups blended tomatoes

1 tbsp sesame tahini

2 tbsp nutritional yeast

1 tbsp Bragg Liquid Soy Seasoning

1 tsp basil

1 tsp thyme

1 tsp chili

1 tsp pink Himalayan salt

1 tbsp vegetable bouillon

Slice eggplant into ¼-inch round pieces. Place on a baking tray, brush with oil and 2 tbsp of soy seasoning. Broil until lightly brown, 3 minutes maximum. Turn and brown other side. Do not leave unattended.

Turn off the broiler and preheat oven to 350°F.

Blend tofu in water and 1 tbsp soy seasoning and set aside.

Meanwhile, make tomato sauce. In a saucepan, simmer blended tomatoes, sesame tahini, nutritional yeast, liquid soy seasoning, basil, thyme, chili, salt, and vegetable bouillon.

Oil a 9x13-inch baking dish. Layer bottom with broiled eggplant. Sprinkle tofu over the eggplant. Add 1 cup of your tomato sauce mixture over first layer. Add second layer of eggplant and tofu, ending with sauce. Sprinkle vegan parmesan cheese to cover top layer. Bake for 40 minutes. Serve hot.

moussaka

1 large eggplant

pinch pink Himalayan salt

½ tsp mint leaves

1 tbsp parsley

1 tbsp maple syrup

¼ tsp cayenne pepper

4 cups tomato sauce

1 cup warm water

1 cup vegan cream cheese

½ tsp oregano

½ tsp basil

½ tsp black pepper

¼ tsp cloves

Preheat oven to 350°F.

Slice the eggplant into ¼-inch thick slices. Lay flat, sprinkle with salt, and cover with paper towels. Place a heavy cutting board on top and press out the water.

In a large saucepan, combine the mint leaves, parsley, maple syrup, cayenne pepper, tomato sauce, and water and simmer for 15 minutes.

To make the cream-cheese topping, melt the vegan cream cheese with the oregano, basil, black pepper, and cloves.

Rinse salt off the eggplant, brush with oil, and brown on both sides in a frying pan. Once browned, place in baking casserole dish. Spoon sauce over eggplant, add cream cheese topping, and bake for 40 minutes.

cabbage rolls

1 cup cooked brown basmati rice

1 medium green cabbage (12 cabbage leaves)

FILLING

1 tbsp avocado oil

1 cup chopped onion

8 mushrooms, peeled and sliced

1 cup mashed tofu

1 clove garlic, minced

1 tbsp pink Himalayan salt and fresh black pepper combined

1 tsp thyme

SAUCE

1 tbsp avocado oil

2 cups tomato sauce

1 tbsp Bragg Liquid Soy Seasoning

1 cup veggie broth

2 tbsp organic corn flour

1 tbsp lemon juice

2 tbsp maple syrup

Have cooked basmati rice and washed cabbage leaves ready. In order for leaves to separate easily but not fall apart, cut out the cabbage heart.

TO MAKE THE FILLING

Sauté all of the ingredients together for 5 minutes.

TO MAKE THE SAUCE

In a separte pan, for the sauce, sauté the avocado oil, tomato sauce, soy seasoning, and veggie broth for 10 minutes. Then stir in the corn flour (to thicken the sauce), lemon juice, and maple syrup.

Preheat oven to 350°F.

Steam cabbage leaves for 10 minutes only. If the stem is very thick, trim it back so the leaves will fold easily. Once steamed, arrange leaves on a baking sheet.

Drop 3-4 tbsp of filling mixture in centre of cabbage leaves. Fold and roll away from you.

Pour a small amount of sauce on the bottom of a 9x13-inch baking dish. Place rolls next to each other in baking dish, and pour sauce over the rolls (retain 1 cup of sauce).

Cover and bake for 40 minutes. Pour a few tablespoons of heated sauce over each roll before serving.

barnyard scalloped potatoes

6 large potatoes, thinly sliced

3 onions, sliced

1 tsp parsley

1 tsp savoury

1 tsp pink Himalayan salt

½ tsp black pepper

1 small green pepper, chopped fine

½ cup nutritional yeast

1 tbsp pea flour

1 tsp paprika

1 tsp powdered sea kelp

2 cups thick coconut milk

Preheat oven to 375°F.

Oil a 9x12-inch oblong pan. Place one layer of sliced potatoes in the bottom of the pan and then a layer of onions (there will be three layers in all).

Sprinkle each layer with parsley, savoury, salt, and black pepper.

Add the chopped green pepper to the midlle layer. For the final layer, start with the onion and top with the potato slices.

Combine the nutritional yeast, pea flour, paprika, and sea kelp and sprinkle over top layer.

Pour the coconut milk over casserole and bake for 40-45 minutes until fork tender. Serve hot!

HINT: For a complete meal, serve with a spinach salad or steamed green beans marinated in apple cider vinegar, olive oil, and Bragg's soy seasoning.

baked brown rice

2 tbsp coconut oil

1 cup finely chopped onion

1 cup finely chopped celery

1 cup brown rice

2½ cups vegetable stock

½ cup grated carrot

½ cup sliced mushrooms

⅛ tsp thyme

⅛ tsp dried marjoram

¾ tsp pink Himalayan salt

⅛ tsp black pepper

Preheat oven to 350°F.

Heat coconut oil in large saucepan. Add onion and celery and stir over medium heat until soft.

Remove from heat, stir in remaining ingredients and pour into an oiled casserole dish.

Cover and bake for 45 minutes.

2½ cups water

1 tbsp organic miso paste

1 cup washed quinoa

½ tsp thyme

½ tsp ginger

½ tsp cumin

1 tsp pink Himalayan salt

½ cup julienne tofu

½ cup julienne carrot

1 medium onion, diced

1 tbsp avocado oil

1 cup peas, fresh or frozen

March Hare quinoa stew

Bring water to a boil. Add miso paste and stir to dissolve into water. Then add quinoa, thyme, ginger, cumin, salt, tofu, carrot, onion, avocado oil, and peas. Bring to a boil, reduce heat to low, cover, and steam for 25 minutes.

Serve in a bowl with a dollop of parsley pesto and a sprinkle of nutritional yeast flakes.

> **COME FROM** Away Piccalilli Relish (page 173) makes a great complement to this dish.

2½ cups water

1 cup millet

1 medium onion, diced

2 tbsp avocado oil

1 cup sliced mushrooms

1 medium organic carrot, diced

¼ cup Bragg Liquid Soy Seasoning

1 tsp basil

1 tsp parsley

1 tsp thyme

1 cup quinoa flakes

1 cup hot vegetable broth

1 cup fresh cut Brussels sprouts or fresh or frozen organic peas

pinch paprika

pinch cayenne pepper

1 Pie Crust That Works (page 116)

millet pie

In a saucepan, bring 2½ cups of water to a boil, add millet and simmer on low for 20 minutes.

In a large frying pan, sauté the onions in the avocado oil. Add mushrooms and carrot. Then add cooked millet along with the soy seasoning, basil, parsley and thyme, and stir well. Cover and let simmer on low heat.

Preheat oven to 350°F.

In a mixing bowl, add the quinoa flakes to hot vegetable broth and allow to sit for 5 minutes. Then stir the much expanded quinoa flakes into the pot of millet.

Finally, add the Brussels sprouts or peas and season with a pinch of paprika and cayenne pepper.

Fill pie crust and put pastry top over millet pie. Make fork holes on top of the pie crust to allow steam to escape.

Bake for 30 minutes.

wild chanterelle stew

2 cups chanterelle mushrooms

1 tbsp vegetable oil

1 large onion, diced

1 celery stalk, diced

½ medium green pepper, chopped

2 cloves garlic, minced

½ tsp oregano

½ tsp thyme

½ tsp savoury

2 cups organic firm tofu, diced

2 medium carrots, diced

3 large new potatoes, cubed large

1 medium parsnip, diced

4 leaves Swiss chard or kale, chopped

1 cup warm water

3 tbsp yellow pea flour

1 cup water

2 tbsp Bragg Liquid Soy Seasoning

Simmer the chanterelles in a cast-iron frying pan on medium heat until liquid escapes from mushrooms. Drain off liquid and discard in your compost. Put mushrooms in a bowl and set aside.

Sauté the following in vegetable oil for five minutes: onion, celery, green pepper, garlic, oregano, thyme, savoury, and tofu. Then add the mushrooms.

Add the carrot, potatoes, parsnip, and Swiss chard. Stir in 1 cup warm water, and stew on medium heat for 10 minutes.

In a measuring cup, combine the yellow pea flour and 1 cup water (gradually) to form a paste. Stir this into bubbling stew until it is well mixed.

Reduce heat to medium-low and add more liquid as needed to make a gravy-like consistency.

Season with soy seasoning. Ready to eat when veggies are fork tender. Be careful not to overcook.

Serve with Quidi Vidi Soup Biscuits (page 92).

tofu style lasagna

1 pkg (454g) lasagna noodles

¼ cup avocado oil

1 large onion, diced

1 large green pepper, diced

2 stalks celery, diced

2 cloves garlic, minced

1 cup peeled and sliced mushrooms

2 cups tomato sauce

6 cups tomatoes, lightly blended

½ tsp oregano

½ tsp basil

½ tsp parsley

1 tsp pink Himalayan salt

32 oz firm tofu, mashed

1 tbsp Bragg Liquid Soy Seasoning

1 tbsp wheat-free soy sauce

2 tbsp lemon juice

2 cups chopped fresh spinach

3 cups grated vegan mozzarella cheese

Preheat oven to 350°F.

Cook lasagna noodles according to package instructions. Add 1 tbsp of olive oil to the boiling water. Drain and cover pasta with cold water. This cools the noodles and prevents them from sticking together.

While noodles are cooking, make the sauce. Sauté in avocado oil, the onion, green pepper, celery, garlic, mushrooms, tomato sauce, and tomatoes. Add oregano, basil, parsley, and salt, and simmer over low heat for 20 minutes.

Mash tofu with the soy seasoning, soy sauce, and lemon juice. Set aside.

In a 9x13-inch lasagna pan, spread a small amount of sauce over the bottom of the pan. Add a layer of cooked lasagna noodles, and a layer of fresh spinach and grated vegan cheese over the noodles.

Spread at least 1 cup of the tofu filling over this layer. Begin again with the tomato sauce, noodles, tofu, spinach and cheese.

End with sauce and top with grated cheese or Nutritional Yeast Sauce (page 171).

Bake for 30 minutes.

scallop (seitan) casserole

1 cup seitan chunks

2 medium onions, diced

1 medium green pepper, diced

1 stalk celery, diced

1 clove garlic, crushed

1 tsp oregano

1 tsp thyme

1 tsp basil

2 tbsp avocado oil

1 cup diced carrot

1 cup julienned green cabbage

2 tbsp Bragg Liquid Soy Seasoning

1 cup water

1 cup coconut milk

2 tbsp organic cornstarch

1 pkg (454g) spinach noodles

If you don't have seitan chunks to use as your scallops, you can also make your own raw gluten as in the Festive Barbeque Gluten recipe (page 138).

Sauté the onions, green pepper, celery, garlic, oregano, thyme, and basil in the avocado oil. Add the seitan and continue to fry until tender and a little golden.

Add carrot and cabbage and simmer for 10-15 minutes, stirring often to prevent sticking. Then add soy seasoning, water, coconut milk, and cornstarch. Casserole should look golden brown.

Meanwhile, cook spinach noodles according to package instructions. Drain the noodles, return them to their pot, and stir in a big dollop of pesto.

Serve casserole over noodles.

GARDEN SALAD (page 42) makes a great side dish for this hearty casserole.

soy loaf (to fill a hole)

4 cups soy pulp or TVP*

2 cups millet flour, quinoa flour and rice flour combination

1 cup wheat germ or quinoa flakes

¾ cup nutritional yeast flakes

2½ tsp ground fennel

1 tbsp black pepper

3 tsp oregano

2 tsp pink Himalayan salt

2 tbsp garlic, minced

2 tbsp prepared mustard

2 tsp allspice

1¼ cup unsweetened coconut milk

¼ cup sesame tamari soy sauce

¼ cup Bragg Liquid Soy Seasoning

Preheat oven to 375°F.

In a large stainless-steel bowl, mix all ingredients well. Oil two 4x8-inch loaf pans, fill with mixture ¾ full, and cover with tinfoil.

Bake for 60 minutes. Remove tinfoil for the final 20 minutes to brown the top of loaf.

Remove from oven and let sit in pans 10 minutes to cool.

Slice and fry as a side dish or mash to use in spaghetti or chili recipes. Will keep in fridge up to 5 days.

tvp Soy pulp or texturized vegetable protein (TVP) is often used in veggie burgers and other plant-based products. It can be purchased at most health-food stores. If you want to make your own, soak 2 cups of organic soy beans overnight. Drain and put beans through a grinder. Bring 8 cups of water to a boil in a large pot and then add the ground soy beans. Simmer for 30 minutes, stirring to prevent sticking. Allow to cool and squeeze the pulp through a cheese cloth to obtain soy milk. Pour soy milk into a glass bottle and refrigerate. The remaining pulp can be used fresh in a loaf, as in this recipe, or spread on a large cookie sheet and baked for 40 minutes at 350°F. The dehydrated TVP can then be cooled and stored in a Mason jar for future use.

everybody's ginger stir-fry

8 oz tofu, cubed

1 tbsp Bragg Liquid Soy Seasoning

1 tbsp minced ginger root

1 tsp pink Himalayan salt

2 tbsp vegetable oil

16 oz fresh broccoli

2 medium onions, cut in wedges

1 cup julienned carrot

½ cup pea pods, fresh or frozen

1 stalk celery, slivered

3 stalks green onions, sliced diagonally

1 cup fresh spinach

¾ cup water

1 tbsp Bragg Liquid Soy Seasoning

1 tbsp organic cornstarch

Marinate cubed tofu in the soy seasoning, minced ginger, and salt for at least 15 minutes. Then, in a wok or cast-iron frying pan, sauté tofu in the vegetable oil.

Add broccoli, onion wedges, and carrot, and stir-fry 1 minute. Then add pea pods, celery, green onions, and spinach. Toss lightly.

Combine water, soy seasoning, and organic cornstarch. Add to cooking vegetables until liquid boils. Reduce heat, cover, and cook for 2-3 minutes, until vegetables are crisp-tender.

DELICIOUS WHEN served over a bed of cooked basmati rice.

pad thai one on

2 tbsp sesame oil

1 cup organic tofu cut into ½ inch cubes

1 medium red bell pepper, julienned

1 carrot, thinly julienned

1 cup broccoli flowerets

1 pkg (545g) rice noodles

¾ cup fresh bean sprouts

1 cup finely chopped roasted peanuts

1tbsp chopped cilantro

DRESSING

¼ cup rice vinegar

¼ cup organic cane sugar

2 tbsp finely chopped basil leaves

3 stems green onions or scallions, thinly sliced

2 cloves garlic, minced

1 tsp chili powder

½ tsp pink Himalayan salt

1 tbsp organic soy sauce

2 tbsp sesame oil

1 tbsp fresh lime juice

Prepare Dressing first and set aside.

In a skillet, sauté the sesame oil, tofu, red bell pepper, carrot, and broccoli.

Meanwhile, cook rice noodles according to package instructions.

Add half of the dressing over the noodles and gently toss to combine. Next add sautéed vegetables and tofu then pour remaining dressing over top. Toss until evenly coated.

Transfer to a large platter. Add bean sprouts and half of the peanuts and toss. Sprinkle with remaining green onions and basil (from dressing), and the remaining peanuts.

Top with fresh cilantro before serving.

TO MAKE THE DRESSING

In a mixing bowl, combine vinegar with organic cane sugar and stir until sugar is dissolved. Then add half of the chopped basil and half of the sliced green onions (reserve the other halves for garnish).

Add garlic, chili powder, salt, and soy sauce then whisk in sesame oil and lime juice until well blended.

chili sans carne

3 cups red kidney beans

10 cups fresh water

2 tbsp avocado oil

1 large onion, diced

1 medium green pepper, diced

2 cloves garlic, minced

2 cups firm tofu, crumbled

1 tbsp chili powder

1 tsp cumin

1 tsp pink Himalayan salt

1 cup diced carrot

1 cup peeled and thinly sliced mushrooms

1 cup organic corn cut from cob

2 cups tomato sauce or 4 medium tomatoes, crushed

Cook the kidney beans in fresh water until soft, about 60 minutes.

In a cast-iron pot, sauté the avocado oil, diced onion, green pepper, garlic, tofu, chili powder, cumin, pink Himalayan salt, diced carrot, mushrooms, corn, and tomato sauce.

Drain and add the cooked beans to the pot with enough sauce to cover the beans. Simmer for 30 minutes.

Serve hot with Cornmeal Buns (page 91) and Baked Brown Rice (page 146).

HINT: Beans cook faster if they have been soaked overnight in a stainless-steel pot or glass bowl. Always discard water after soaking.

dandelion scoff

2 cups fresh wild dandelion leaves

2 cups quartered potatoes

1 cup sliced carrot

1 cup sliced parsnip

1 cup cubed small turnip

1 medium onion, quartered

A traditional Newfoundland dandelion scoff.

Make sure your dandelion leaves are washed well and separated from their stems. Parboil for 5 minutes in a pot of boiling water.

Meanwhile prepare your pot of vegetables, steaming the potatoes, carrot, parsnip, turnip, and onion for 15 minutes.

Add more liquid to the pot of vegetables, and then add dandelion to the top of the steaming pot and continue to steam for another 20 minutes or until vegetables and dandelion are tender.

Serve with Pagan Vegan Gravy (page 171).

stuffed zucchini

1 medium zucchini

1 cup cooked millet

1 cup sliced onion

⅔ cup chopped fresh green beans

1 cup coarsely chopped spinach

1 tbsp roasted sesame seeds

¼ cup pine nuts

1 cup chopped mushroom

1 tbsp millet flour

1 tsp lemon zest

1 tsp thyme

1 tsp basil

1 tsp pink Himalayan salt

Preheat oven to 400°F.

Split zucchini down the middle, length wise, but not all the way to the bottom peel. Open like a book and carefully scoop out seeds.

Mix the cooked millet with all remaining ingredients to create the filling for the zucchini.

Stuff the zucchini with filling. Close the zucchini and secure with kitchen twine. Place in baking dish and bake until fork tender, about 30 minutes.

Remove from oven and place on a large platter. Surround with sprigs of fresh parsley and wedges of baked potatoes. Serve with fresh pesto (page 37).

how to cook millet

1 cup raw hulled millet
3 cups boiling water
¼ tsp sea salt
1 tbsp vegetable oil

Rinse and pour millet into a saucepan. Add boiling water, sea salt, and oil. Bring to a boil, lower heat, cover, and simmer until all liquid is absorbed (about 20 minutes).

more than a pot pie

1 onion, diced

1 cup diced parsnip

2 carrots, diced

2 stalks celery, diced

2 cups diced baby new potatoes

1 cup sliced kale

1 tsp thyme

1 tsp savoury

1 bay leaf (remove before serving)

2 tbsp avocado oil

DOUGH

3 cups flour

½ tsp baking soda

1 tsp baking powder

1 cup unsweetened almond milk

1 tbsp vegetable bouillon cube dissolved in ½ cup hot water

⅓ cup avocado oil

PEA FLOUR THICKENING

1 tsp Himalayan salt

3 tbsp yellow pea flour

1 cup warm water

1 cup peas, fresh or frozen

Preheat oven to 350°F.

In a cast-iron pot or Dutch oven, sauté the onion, parsnip, carrots, celery, potatoes, kale, thyme, savoury, and bay leaf in 2 tbsp of avocado oil. Let simmer on low heat while you make the pot-pie crust.

TO MAKE THE DOUGH

In a large mixing bowl, combine the flour, baking soda, baking powder, almond milk, dissolved vegetable bouillon, and ⅓ cup avocado oil. Mix until well combined, and set dough aside.

TO MAKE THE PEA FLOUR THICKENING

Make the pea flour thickening in a measuring cup. First combine the salt and yellow pea flour. Gradually add warm water (up to 1 cup) to make a paste. Pour this smooth mixture into the simmering pot of vegetables. Stir as it thickens fast. Add more water if needed. Add peas.

Spoon dough over top of the hot pie and bake for 30 minutes.

🌱 **SAVOURY IS** a traditional herb originally from the Mediterranean, but there is nothing quite like Mt. Scio Farm Savoury, grown right here in Newfoundland. It has its own distinct flavour, and it really does make all the difference

fettuccini in a Marian White sauce

½ cup diced onion

½ cup chopped celery

2 tbsp avocado oil

2 tbsp vegetable bouillon seasoning

½ tsp savoury

½ tsp thyme

2 cloves garlic, minced

2 cups organic tofu or tempeh, diced

1 cup short carrot sticks

1 cup fresh chopped broccoli

1 pkg (454g) fettuccini spinach noodles

¼ cup yellow pea flour

2 cups unsweetened coconut milk

1 cup spring water

½ tbsp finely chopped fresh parsley

1 tbsp Bragg Liquid Soy Seasoning

Sauté the onion and celery in the avocado oil, vegetable bouillon seasoning, savoury, thyme, garlic, and tofu. Fry on medium-low heat for 5 minutes, stirring to prevent sticking.

Add carrot sticks and broccoli. Reduce heat and simmer for 5 minutes.

Meanwhile, in a large pot, cook fettuccini spinach noodles according to package instructions.

Add the yellow pea flour to a measuring cup and stir in coconut milk. When smooth, add this mixture to the sautéed ingredients. Continue stirring on low heat until thick and creamy. As it thickens, you can add up to 1 cup spring water.

Remove sauce from heat and stir in parsley and mineral bouillon. Stir cooked noodles into the sauce.

Serve immediately with a dollop of pesto over each serving.

Sandrosco's chickpea festive loaf

4 cups chickpeas

2 tbsp avocado oil

2 cups diced onion

1 stalk celery, diced

½ cup diced green pepper

2 cloves garlic, minced

1 cup sesame tahini

1 tbsp garden thyme

1 tbsp savoury

1 tbsp organic vegetable cube

¼ cup dried parsley

1 bay leaf

½ loaf rice bread

½ cup Bragg Liquid Soy Seasoning

1 tsp pink Himalayan salt

Wash and soak the chickpeas in water overnight. Discard water and replace with fresh water, enough to cover. Cook until soft (takes 2-3 hours). Drain and grind chickpeas in a food processor.

Preheat oven to 325°F.

Sauté the avocado oil, diced onion, celery, green pepper, and garlic. Then add tahini, thyme, savoury, vegetable cube, dried parsley, and bay leaf, and fry.

In a separate bowl, grate the rice bread into crumbs. Then add enough hot water to cover crumbs and season with soy seasoning and salt.

Remove the bay leaf from the sautéed mixture. Combine the bread crumbs, sautéed mixture, and ground chickpeas.

Pour into oiled loaf pan (makes a 2-inch high loaf). Cover and bake for 90 minutes.

Serve with Pagan Vegan Gravy (page 171), fresh steamed vegetables, and cranberry sauce.

HINT: Reserve some of your chickpea water. It acts like egg whites when whipped, so it works great in a meringue or mousse.

belly full baked beans

2 cups organic navy beans

4 cups water (approx.)

2 medium onions, thinly sliced

1 tbsp Bragg Liquid Soy Seasoning

¼ cup apple cider vinegar

1 tbsp organic yellow mustard

1 tbsp maple syrup

½ cup blackstrap molasses

1 cup tomato paste or 1 cup organic ketchup

¼ tsp organic fresh cracked black pepper

1 tbsp vegetable bouillon cube dissolved in ¼ cup hot water

Wash the beans and remove any spoiled ones. Soak overnight in about 4 cups of water.

Drain the water from the beans. Pour the beans into a cast-iron pot, cover with fresh water, and bring to a boil. Partially cover the pot and cook on medium heat for 45 minutes. Let sit in hot water while you prepare the sauce. Keep in mind that it is in soaking and boiling the beans that they get soft. Baking seasons the beans.

Spread the thinly sliced onions along bottom of bean crock.

In a 2-cup measuring cup, mix the soy seasoning, apple cider vinegar, mustard, maple syrup, blackstrap molasses, tomato paste, black pepper, and dissolved bouillon.

Once beans are soft, drain the water.

Preheat oven to 250°F.

Pour sauce over onions and place beans over the sauce. Do not stir. Pour in just enough hot water to cover beans. Cover crock and bake for 7 hours.

At end of 4 hours, remove 1 cup of beans, mash, and stir into other beans. Put thin slices of tofu or tempeh on top of beans (optional). Add water as needed to keep beans moist.

Remove cover for the final hour to brown the beans.

Serve with Cornbread (page 91).

tofu and spinach quiche

3 cups crumbled firm organic tofu

2 tbsp oil

2 medium onion, diced

1 medium carrot, grated

4 pieces sun-dried tomato, cut small

½ cup nutritional yeast

3 tbsp fresh lemon juice

2 tbsp Bragg Liquid Soy Seasoning

1 tbsp prepared mustard

2 cloves garlic, crushed

½ tsp fresh cracked black pepper

1 tbsp vegetable bouillon cube dissolved in 2 tbsp hot water

1 tsp thyme

1 tbsp fresh basil or pesto

3 cups fresh chopped organic spinach

1 cup vegan grated Gouda cheese

1 unbaked 8-inch pie shell

Preheat oven to 400°F.

Using a deep cast-iron pot, sauté oil, onion, carrot, sun-dried tomato, nutritional yeast, fresh lemon juice, soy seasoning, mustard, garlic, pepper, dissolved vegetable bouillon, thyme, and basil.

Add finely crumbled tofu and continue to sauté for 5 more minutes then add spinach and vegan Gouda.

Pour mixture into pie shell and bake for 45 minutes. Allow to cool 5 minutes before serving.

saucy peanut sauce
(for rice noodles)

1 pkg (454g) rice noodles

¾ cup roasted peanuts

3 cloves garlic

3 tbsp soy sauce

3 tbsp apple cider vinegar

1 tbsp maple syrup

1 tbsp hot Dijon mustard

1 tsp cayenne pepper

½ cup light oil, peanut or avocado

½ cup water

1 tbsp sesame oil

2 cups of unsweetened coconut milk

Prepare rice noodles according to package instructions.

Blend the peanuts, garlic, soy sauce, vinegar, maple syrup, mustard, cayenne, light oil, water, and sesame oil for 1 minute. Pour into a saucepan and bring to a bubble over medium heat, stirring often to prevent sticking. Reduce heat and simmer.

Add up to 2 cups of unsweetened coconut milk.

If sauce is too thick, add a few tablespoons of warm water. Mix a few tablespoons of sauce through the noodles before serving.

Pour remaining sauce over plated rice noodles.

HINT: You can also add lightly steamed vegetables, such as carrot and broccoli, to the sauce before pouring over noodles.

1 cup organic long grain brown rice or basmati rice

2 cups water

1 tbsp sesame tahini

1 tsp pink Himalayan salt (optional)

2 tbsp avocado oil

1 medium onion, thinly sliced

2 cloves garlic, crushed

1 stalk celery, chopped

1 small green pepper, diced

2 medium carrots, thinly sliced

4 medium potatoes, cubed

1 medium cauliflower, divided into bite-size florets

1 cup fresh peas

1 cup diced organic tomato

½ cup water

1 tbsp Bragg Liquid Soy Seasoning

SPICE MIX

1 tbsp cumin

1 tbsp coriander

1 tbsp ginger

1 tbsp Jamaican curry

1 tbsp Madras curry

1 tbsp turmeric

2 tbsp organic vegetable bouillon dissolved in 2 tbsp of hot water

1 tsp cayenne pepper

1 tsp pink Himalayan salt

karmafree vegetable curry

Combine the Spice Mix ingredients in a small bowl and set aside.

In a large saucepan, bring 2 cups of water to a boil. Add the rice and, using a fork, stir in the tahini and salt (optional). Cover and cook on low heat for 50 minutes.

Sauté the avocado oil, onion, garlic, celery, and green pepper. Then add the prepared Spice Mix all at once, stir well, and simmer on a low heat for 5 minutes, stirring often. Next add the carrot and potato and simmer for 20 minutes until vegetables are softening. Add cauliflower, peas, and tomato. Stir often with a wooden spoon to prevent curry from sticking to the pot. You can add up to a ½ cup of water to keep curry moist.

Add soy seasoning last. Serve over a bed of cooked brown rice.

MANGO CHUTNEY or coriander chutney make great complements to this curry.

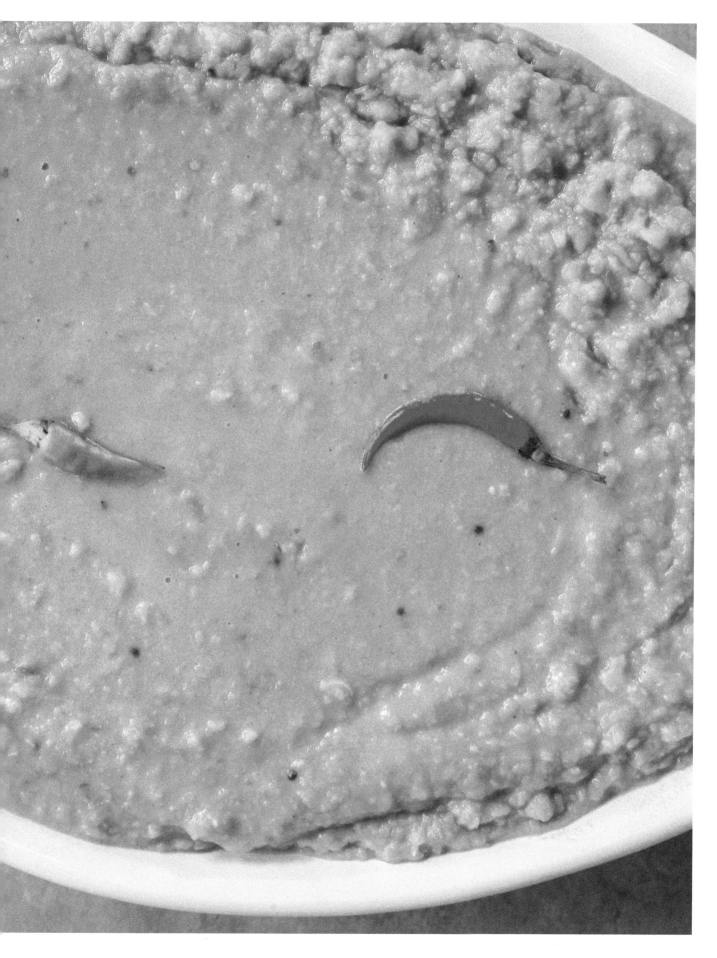

trimmings ▸

pagan vegan gravy

2 tbsp light oil

1 large onion, minced

2 cloves garlic, minced

1 tsp thyme

1 tsp savoury

2 tbsp Bernard Jensen's Protein Seasoning (or ½ tsp pink Himalayan salt)

4 heaping tbsp yellow pea flour

1 cup room-temperature water

2 cups steamed vegetable water

1 tsp Bragg Liquid Soy Seasoning

2 tbsp tomato paste or organic ketchup (optional)

Almost every vegan I know has made their own version of this tasty gravy that can be served over a variety of steamed vegetables and other dishes.

In 2 tbsp of light oil, sauté the onion, garlic, thyme, savoury, and Bernard Jensen's Protein Seasoning. This protein seasoning is the special ingredient that gives the gravy its rich flavour. However, if you cannot find this illusive seasoning, use ½ tsp Himalayan salt or Newfoundland sea salt. Stir with a wooden spoon until the seasoning is absorbed by the oil, onions, and garlic.

In a measuring cup, mix the pea flour with 1 cup of room-temperature water until all lumps have disappeared. Add this to the sautéed ingredients. Gravy will thicken quickly.

If you're adding steamed vegetables to your meal, save the steaming water and add it to your gravy. If not, use up to 2 cups of hot spring water.

Continue stirring to obtain a smooth gravy consistency. When gravy is thick, add the soy seasoning or soy sauce.

Ready to serve wherever you need gravy. Yum!

HINT: If you prefer darker gravy, add 2 tbsp of tomato paste or 2 tbsp of organic ketchup.

nutritional yeast sauce

1 cup nutritional yeast flakes

½ cup apple cider vinegar

1 tbsp organic yellow mustard

1 tsp Himalayan salt

Combine all of the ingredients and add just enough water to make a creamy consistency to pour over your baked dish.

rice dumplings

1 cup rice flour

½ cup coconut flour

1 cup cooked rice

1 tsp Himalayan salt

2 tsp non-alum baking powder

1 tbsp coconut sugar

2 tbsp melted coconut oil

⅔ cup coconut milk

Mix the flours, rice, salt, baking powder, and sugar in a mixing bowl.

Cut in oil until the mixture reaches the consistency of meal.

Stir in milk to make a sticky dough.

Dust a large spoon with flour and spoon 8-10 dumplings into simmering stew, spacing evenly. Cover pot tightly and simmer, without lifting lid, for 15 minutes.

Serve while hot.

tofu coating
(for baking or frying)

1 cup rice flour

1 tsp fresh cracked pepper

½ tsp basil

½ tsp ginger

1 tsp sea salt

1 tbsp paprika

1 tsp dry mustard

½ tsp thyme

½ tsp oregano

1 tbsp chili powder

16 oz firm tofu

½ cup unsweetened coconut milk

½ cup coconut oil

Combine the rice flour, pepper, basil, ginger, sea salt, paprika, dry mustard, thyme, oregano, and chili powder, and spread over a plate or wooden cutting board for rolling.

Slice the tofu into ⅛-inch thick slices. Dip each slice in coconut milk and then roll in the dry mixture.

Heat the coconut oil and deep fry the coated tofu, on each side, for 1 minute until brown.

variation 1: Dip potato wedges into water and then into the coating mixture. Deep fry until golden brown on both sides.

variation 2: To make Tofu Pups or Tofu Veggie Dogs, dip the tofu into flour, then in coconut milk, then into coating mixture. Deep fry and serve on a stick!

come from away piccalilli relish

2 cups chopped green tomatoes

2 cups chopped red pepper

2 cups chopped green pepper

2 cups chopped hot pepper

2 cups chopped onion

1 small cabbage, cored and chopped

1 tsp pink Himalayan salt

1 cup coconut sugar

1 tbsp mustard seed

1 tbsp celery seed

2 cups apple cider vinegar

1 cup Quebec maple syrup

In a large pot, bring the tomatoes, red pepper, green pepper, hot pepper, onion, cabbage, salt, coconut sugar, mustard seed, celery seed, and apple cider vinegar to a boil.

Reduce heat and cook for 30 minutes, stirring occasionally until thick.

Ladle into hot Mason jars, leaving ½-inch of head space.

Pour syrup into each jar, covering veggies and leaving ¼-inch head space. Cover jars.

Immerse jars in boiling water for 10 minutes. Remove from heat. Cool and check seals.

Label and store in a cool, dry place.

no fuss chips

6 large potatoes, sliced

¼ cup olive oil

2 tbsp nutritional yeast flakes

1 tbsp apple cider vinegar

1 tsp pink Himalayan salt

Preheat oven to 400°F.

Scrub and slice 6 large potatoes as you would for French fries.

Remove middle rack from oven, brush clean, and spread your fries directly on the rack.

Bake for 30 minutes (or until browned and slightly crispy). Remove from oven with a spatula and put in a stainless-steel bowl.

Toss with olive oil, nutritional yeast flakes, apple cider vinegar, and salt.

HINT: You can also make traditional Dollar and Cents Chips by cutting potato into thin round slices.

stuffing
for its own sake

½ loaf of not-so-fresh rice or
spelt bread

1½ tbsp savoury

1 tsp thyme

1 medium onion, chopped fine

1½ tbsp coconut or olive oil

1 tsp pink Himalayan salt

Preheat oven to 350°F.

Blend or grate by hand the ½ loaf of bread into a stainless-steel mixing bowl.

Add the savoury, thyme, onion, oil, and salt. Mix together by hand.

Place in an oiled casserole dish, cover, and bake for 20 minutes.

devilled eggless
sandwich

¼ cup sliced green onion

¼ cup finely chopped celery

1 tsp sea salt

1 cup mashed medium to firm tofu

½ cup vegenaise

½ cup tofu

1 tsp oil

1 tbsp Bragg Liquid Soy Seasoning

1 clove garlic, minced

Dijon mustard and vegenaise to
spread

4 slices of spelt or protein bread

Alfalfa sprouts or lettuce

Add the green onion, celery, and salt to the mashed tofu. Then fold in the ½ cup of vegenaise.

Hand blend ½ cup of tofu with the oil, soy seasoning, and garlic. Then mix well with the mashed tofu.

Spread Dijon mustard and a little vegenaise on the four slices of bread. Spoon mashed tofu spread onto the bread. Place alfalfa sprouts or a leaf of lettuce on top.

Goes great with fresh carrot juice!

la socca crêpe de nice

2 cups chickpea flour

2 cups water

½ cup extra-virgin olive oil

1 tsp pink Himalayan salt

1 tsp thyme

This tasty savoury dish is a specialty from Nice in the south of France. I have had the pleasure of enjoying it in a Nice market. Socca is normally made outdoors in a clay oven, but a very hot oven will do: wood stoves work best.

Whisk flour, water, ¼ extra-virgin olive oil, sat, and thyme to form a light batter and let rest for 30 minutes to let the ingredients cream together.

Preheat oven to 475°F. Place a 10-inch cast-iron pan or equivalent baking sheet into the oven to warm.

Once the oven is preheated, remove the pan from oven and coat the bottom with olive oil.

Whisk batter one last time. Pour batter evenly onto crepe pan about one inch thick, no more.

Dribble ¼ cup olive oil over the surface of the socca.

Put your oven on broil. Place the pan at least 4 to 6 inches below the broiler, and broil for 5 minutes. Check often to make sure it is not burning.

Broil another few minutes until socca is light brown on top, cooked in the middle, and crisp on the edges.

Use a spatula to remove from the pan. Serve piping hot. Yum!

> **SOCCA CAN** be dressed with pesto and used as a pizza crust or served as bread with salad. It is as versatile as you care to make it.

desserts

bitesize friday night ginger delights

Yields 2 dozen cookies

¼ cup sunflower oil

1 cup coconut sugar

1 tbsp egg replacer mixed with ¼ cup water

¼ cup mild flavoured molasses

½ tsp pure vanilla

¼ tsp pink Himalayan salt

½ tsp cloves

1 tsp cinnamon

2 tbsp ground ginger

2 cups all-purpose flour

1 tsp baking soda

Preheat oven to 350°F.

Combine and mix the sunflower oil, coconut sugar, egg replacer mixed with water, molasses, and vanilla until smooth.

In a separate bowl, mix the salt, cloves, cinnamon, ginger, flour, and baking soda with a wooden spoon.

Combine the wet mixture with the dry and stir for two minutes until smooth. Let sit for 10 minutes to thicken.

Drop by the tablespoon onto an oiled cookie sheet, sprinkle with organic sugar, and then imprint each Delight with a fork.

Bake for 15 minutes. Cookies will be soft when first taken from the oven, but will harden as they cool. If you prefer a softer cookie, bake for 12 minutes.

Allow to cool for 5 minutes before removing to a cooling rack.

HINT: When imprinting your Delights, dip your fork in water first to prevent sticking.

hearty quinoa and raisin cookies

Yields 20 cookies

1 cup organic raisins

½ cup spring water

1 cup flour

½ tsp baking soda

1 tsp baking powder

dash pink Himalayan salt

1 cup quinoa flakes

1 cup coconut sugar

½ cup almond butter

1 tsp organic vanilla

½ cup melted coconut oil

1 tbsp flax meal mixed with 3 tbsp water

½ cup crushed walnuts

Soak the raisins in the spring water for at least 30 minutes. Then drain the raisins, but retain the water.

Preheat oven to 350°F.

In a bowl, combine the flour, baking soda, baking powder, Himalayan salt, quinoa flakes, and coconut sugar.

In a separate bowl, combine the raisin water, vanilla, coconut oil, and flax meal mixture.

Combine and stir the liquid mixture with the dry ingredients. Stir in raisins and walnuts. Let sit 10 minutes to allow quinoa to expand.

Drop individual cookies by the tablespoon onto a lightly oiled baking sheet.

Bake for 18-20 minutes until brown. Let cool 5 minutes before removing to a cooling rack.

HINT: You can use pecans instead of walnuts, or for something even crunchier, use coconut strips.

Mila's peanut butter gems

Yields about 2 dozen gems

2 cups all-purpose wheat-free flour

1 tsp baking powder

½ tsp baking soda

½ tsp pink Himalayan salt

½ cup pure maple syrup

½ cup organic coconut sugar

½ cup melted coconut oil

½ cup coconut milk

1 heaping tbsp of egg replacer mixed with ¼ cup water

1 tsp pure vanilla

1 cup organic peanut butter or no-nut butter

Preheat oven to 350°F.

In a bowl, combine the flour, baking powder, baking soda, and salt.

In a large measuring cup, cream together the maple syrup, coconut sugar, coconut oil, coconut milk, egg replacer mixed with water, pure vanilla, and peanut butter.

Combine dry ingredients with liquid ingredients. The batter should be fairly stiff.

Drop by small spoonfuls onto an oiled cookie sheet and press lightly with fork. You can dip the fork in water to prevent batter from sticking.

Bake for 13 minutes. Watch them closely because they cook quickly. Allow to cool before removing from cookie sheet or you will end up with a cookie crumble.

Ella's first-grade Valentine surprise cookies

Yields 16 cookies

½ cup light oil

½ cup coconut water or milk

1 cup coconut sugar

2 cups light flour

1 tbsp organic cinnamon

1 tbsp no-alum baking powder

1 cup dark chocolate chips

Preheat oven to 350°F.

In a measuring cup, stir together the oil, coconut water, and melted coconut oil.

In a bowl, combine the coconut sugar, flour, cinnamon, and baking powder.

Combine the dry ingredients with the wet ingredients. Stir until thick, adding up to ½ cup more flour for extra firm cookies. Stir in chocolate chips.

Flatten on a floured wooden board until about ½-inch thick and cut into 2-inch hearts.

Bake for 18 minutes on an oiled cookie sheet.

Spread homemade raspberry jelly on cooled cookies.

CHOCOLATE FROSTING (page 186) gives these cookies a tasty and festive flare.

[apricot pudding]

apricot coconut drop cookies

Yields 12 drop cookies

6 organic dried apricots

1 cup coconut flour

1 cup spelt flour

1 cup organic coconut sugar

½ tsp pink Himalayan salt

1 tbsp no-alum baking powder

½ tsp baking soda

1 tbsp egg replacer mixed with
¼ cup water

¼ cup melted coconut oil

1 cup organic coconut milk

1 tbsp fresh lemon juice

1 tsp cinnamon

1 tbsp coconut sugar

Preheat oven to 400°F. Cut each apricot in half and set the 12 pieces aside.

In a bowl, mix the coconut flour, spelt flour, coconut sugar, salt, baking powder, and baking soda.

In a separate bowl, whisk together the egg replacer mixed with water, melted coconut oil, coconut milk, and lemon juice. Then stir into dry ingredients, but do not over stir.

Reserve ½ cup of cookie dough for the top of cookies. Place a heaping tablespoonful of cookie dough, per cookie, onto an oiled baking sheet. Press ½ apricot into the center of each cookie. Then top with enough of the reserved dough to cover the apricot. Sprinkle cinnamon and coconut sugar on top.

Bake for 15 minutes. Serve warm with tea and a friend.

SULPHUR DIOXIDE is a food preservative used to keep an apricot's original colour. However, organic apricots are unsulfured, so they are darker, but have lots of flavour.

apricot pudding

2 cups organic dried apricots

5 cups water

1 cup coconut sugar

2 tbsp arrowroot flour

Soak the dried apricots in cold water overnight or in warm water for at least 4 hours.

Bring the 5 cups of water and coconut sugar to a boil. Add soaked apricots (retain apricot water for later). Blend the mixture in a food processor with the arrowroot flour.

Return to heat and stir in ½ cup apricot water (left over from soaking). Bring to a boil, stirring constantly for 3 minutes or until thick.

Spoon into dessert dishes and chill. Serve with coconut whipped cream or soy cream.

Greg's fashionable lemon-pineapple squares

CRUST

2 cup wheat-free granola (no raisins or fruit)

½ cup rice flour

½ cup coconut flour

½ cup coconut oil

2 tbsp water

FILLING

5 cups unsweetened pineapple juice

juice of 2 lemons

zest of 1 lemon

½ cup pure maple syrup

¾ cup ground almonds

7 heaping tbsp arrowroot flour

TO MAKE THE CRUST

Preheat oven to 350°F.

Combine the granola, rice flour, and coconut flour. Then mix in the coconut oil and crumble the mixture with your hands. Sprinkle 2 tbsp of water over this and press into a 9 x 13-inch baking pan. Prick holes in bottom and bake for 15 minutes.

TO MAKE THE FILLING

While crust is baking, prepare your filling. Depending on the size of your blender, you may need to divide the liquid into two parts to avoid spillage. Blend the unsweetened pineapple juice, lemon juice, lemon zest, and maple syrup. Blend for 1 minute.

Add the almonds and arrowroot flour to blender and continue to blend for 1 more minute.

Pour into a thick-bottomed pot or boiler. Bring to a boil. Reduce heat to low, and stir constantly for 5-10 minutes until thick.

Remove crust from oven and pour the filling over crust to ¼-inch thickness.

Place in refrigerator and thoroughly cool (at least 4 hours) before cutting into squares. Use a spatula to remove squares from pan.

Before serving, top with coconut whipped cream or soy cream.

Elly Danica's pear tart

1 tsp ginger

1 tsp cinnamon

¼ tsp sea salt

1 cup raw cane sugar

½ cup almond meal

1½ cups wheat-free flour combination

1 tbsp arrowroot flour

¼ cup almond milk

2 cups peeled and sliced fresh pears

1 tbsp melted coconut oil

This is a throwback to the 1990s, when Elly visited me in St. John's and made a variation of this tart. She enjoyed my combination of flours and had never cooked with coconut oil.

Preheat oven to 350°F.

Combine all the dry ingredients and then mix in the almond milk. Fold sliced pears into the batter.

Smear a 9-inch round springfoam cake pan with oil, and sprinkle lightly with cornmeal. Elly turned the pan over a sink and tapped it to loosen excess crumbs.

Put batter in pan and level off with a spatula. Dribble melted coconut oil over tart.

Bake for 50 minutes or until top has become a light golden brown.

When tart is done, but still warm, loosen from pan and transfer to platter. Tart should have a near pudding texture. Serve with a raspberry coulis or unaccompanied while warm.

guilt-ridden chocolate frosting from the bay

8 tbsp grated dark chocolate

1 cup coconut milk

1 cup raw coconut sugar

⅛ tsp Himalayan salt

1 tbsp coconut oil

½ tsp pure organic vanilla

In a medium saucepan, melt the chocolate with ¼ cup coconut milk. Whisk in coconut sugar and salt. Stirring constantly, gradually add the remaining coconut milk and coconut oil.

Bring to a boil over medium heat, stirring constantly. Reduce heat, but mixture should continue to bubble.

Remove from heat and add the vanilla. Place saucepan in cold water, let stand 4 minutes without stirring. Remove from cold water.

Beat for about 5 minutes until the mixture thickens.

Chill for 1 hour.

Delicious when spread over any cake or cookie.

HINT: Use a thick-bottomed saucepan to melt the chocolate. Dip a knife in cold water to aide in spreading the frosting.

welcome home blueberry bake

2 cups spelt flour (or your combination of wheat-free flours)

1 tbsp no-alum baking powder

1 tbsp cinnamon

½ tsp nutmeg

½ cup coconut sugar

½ cup melted coconut oil

½ cup applesauce

¾ cup coconut milk

1 cup fresh blueberries

SAUCE

1 cup coconut cream

2 tbsp maple syrup

1 tsp pure vanilla

1 tbsp arrowroot flour

1 tsp water

Preheat oven to 350°F.

In a stainless-steel bowl, combine spelt flour, baking powder, cinnamon, nutmeg, and coconut sugar.

In a separate bowl, combine the coconut oil, applesauce, and coconut milk. Then mix the wet ingredients with the dry ingredients and fold in blueberries last.

Spread over an 8-inch square baking pan, and bake for 30 minutes.

Remove from oven and allow to cool in the pan. Do not cut until cool, unless you want a pudding!

TO MAKE THE SAUCE

While squares are cooling, you can conjure up the sauce. In a medium saucepan, heat and melt the coconut cream, maple syrup, and pure vanilla. Hand blend the arrowroot flour with 1 tsp water, mixing until smooth, before adding to cream. Cool in refrigerator for 30 minutes before pouring over blueberry bake.

➤ **YOU CAN** replace applesauce with crushed pineapple.

Eldamar blueberry blunt

1 tbsp egg replacer mixed with ¼ cup water

¼ cup sunflower oil

½ cup coconut milk

½ cup pure maple syrup

2 cups spelt flour or any wheat-free combination

2 tsp no-alum baking powder

1 tsp each cinnamon

1 tsp ginger

¼ tsp sea salt

2 cups fresh blueberries

2 tbsp arrowroot flour

2 tsp fresh lemon juice

¼ cup coconut sugar

Not unlike a traditional East Coast blueberry grunt, this blunt is made with a little more laissez-faire.

Preheat oven to 350°F.

In a large bowl, cream together the egg replacer mixed with water, sunflower oil, coconut milk, and maple syrup.

In a separate bowl, combine the spelt flour, baking powder, cinnamon, ginger, and salt. Stir this mixture into the wet ingredients.

Lightly oil the bottom and sides of a 5x8-inch pan. Line bottom with blueberries. Sprinkle the arrowroot flour through berries. Then squeeze the lemon juice over berries, and finally sprinkle with coconut sugar.

Pour batter over berries. Bake for 35-40 minutes or until berries bubble through.

Flip the individual servings onto dishes so the blueberries will be on top, and serve with coconut or ice cream.

TRADITIONALLY, A grunt was made on the stove top in a covered cast-iron pan. This blunt also works on the stove top, but keep the lid on tight for 15 minutes.

Avondale blueberry dash

2 cups all-purpose flour

1 tbsp no-alum baking powder

1 cup organic coconut sugar

1 tbsp egg replacer mixed with ¼ cup water

½ cup avocado oil

½ cup almond milk

1½ cup fresh blueberries

Preheat oven to 350°F.

In a stainless-steel bowl, combine the flour, baking powder, and sugar.

In a second bowl, whisk together the egg replacer and water, avocado oil, and almond milk.

Combine dry ingredients with wet ingredients, and then fold in blueberries.

Spread over a lightly oiled 8x8-inch pan and bake for 30-40 minutes.

While warm, spoon into serving bowls and top with coconut cream.

ginger-pineapple bake for Miko

½ cup maple syrup

1 cup fresh pineapple

½ cup pineapple juice

1½ cups wheat-free, all-purpose flour

1 tsp ginger powder

1 tsp cinnamon

½ tsp allspice

½ tsp cloves

1 tbsp no-alum baking powder

Preheat oven to 350°F.

Blend the maple syrup, pineapple, and pineapple juice. Set aside.

In a bowl, thoroughly hand mix the flour, ginger, cinnamon, allspice, cloves, and baking powder, and then add to blended mixture.

Pour into an 8x8-inch pan.

Bake for 30 minutes. Allow to cool before cutting. Serve with fresh coconut or soy cream.

✿ IN A pinch, you can replace the fresh pineapple with unsweetened canned pineapple.

Dock Ridge partridge berry bog

1 cup unpeeled, thinly sliced apple

2 cups partridge berries

1 cup coconut sugar

1 tbsp arrowroot flour

1 cup all-purpose flour

½ cup coconut flour

2 tsp baking powder

½ cup coconut sugar

¼ tsp sea salt

1 tbsp flax meal

1 cup almond or coconut milk

1 tsp pure vanilla

Preheat oven to 375°F.

Arrange the apple slices and partridge berries over the bottom of an oiled 9x9-inch glass baking dish. Sprinkle with coconut sugar, and dust arrowroot flour through the apples and berries.

In a mixing bowl, combine the flour, coconut flour, baking powder, coconut sugar, salt, and flax meal. Then stir in the almond milk and pure vanilla. Pour the mixture over the apples and berries.

Bake for 40 minutes.

spring delight strawberry-rhubarb crisp

3½ cups sliced fresh rhubarb

3½ cups sliced organic strawberries

2 tbsp fresh lemon juice

2 tbsp organic cornstarch

2 tbsp orange zest

½ cup organic coconut sugar

½ cup quinoa flakes

½ cup coconut flour

1 cup all-purpose flour

¾ cup coconut sugar

2 tsp ground cinnamon

½ cup vegan butter

Preheat oven to 350°F.

Slice your rhubarb into 1-inch thick pieces and cover with water while you prepare your other ingredients.

In a mixing bowl, combine strawberries, lemon juice, cornstarch, orange zest, and coconut sugar. Drain the rhubarb and add it to the mix.

Spread the above mixture into a lightly oiled 8x13-inch baking pan.

In a second bowl, mix the quinoa flakes, coconut flour, all-purpose flour, coconut sugar, and cinnamon. Then cut in vegan butter and crumble with hands. Sprinkle over the strawberry-rhubarb mixture to coat the pan.

Bake for 40 minutes or until fruit is bubbling through. Crust is done when light brown.

Cool on wire rack for 15-20 minutes. Serve with coconut ice cream.

non-traditional strawberry shortcake

Yields a dozen shortcakes

3 cups fresh organic strawberries

½ cup pure maple syrup

2 cups sifted light flour

1 tbsp baking powder

½ tsp sea salt

2 tbsp raw organic cane sugar

½ cup sunflower oil

¾ cup almond milk

1 tsp pure organic vanilla

1 tbsp pure maple syrup

1½ cups prepared coconut or soy cream

Preheat oven to 425°F.

Rinse and hull your strawberries. Reserve 6 whole berries, cut in half, for garnish, and mash the remainder. Place mashed berries in a medium bowl and sprinkle raw cane sugar over top. Set aside until serving time.

In a large bowl, sift together flour, baking powder, sea salt, and cane sugar. Cut in oil until mixture resembles fine crumbs. Slowly add almond milk until flour is evenly moistened. Add vanilla. Do not overmix.

Drop by a heaping tablespoonful (2 inches apart) on an oiled cookie sheet. Bake for 12-14 minutes or until golden brown.

Once shortcakes have been removed from oven, slice each one in half horizontally. Remove the top and place one cake layer on a round serving platter with the cut side facing up. Spoon on mashed berries. Place the top of the shortcake over the berries.

Top with coconut cream and garnish with cut strawberries. Serve warm with a drizzle of pure maple syrup over each and every cake.

FOR VARIATION, this is also very tasty with fresh summer raspberries.

Christmas pudding bubbles brown

½ cup maple syrup

½ cup sunflower oil

½ cup almond milk

½ cup mild flavoured molasses

2 tsp liquid lecithin or flax meal

1 cup seedless organic raisins

1 cup chopped figs or dates

3 cups all-purpose flour

1 tbsp cinnamon

1 tsp ginger

1 tsp nutmeg

1 tsp cloves

1 tbsp orange zest

1 tbsp no-alum baking powder

½ cup slivered almonds

In a large bowl, hand mix the maple syrup and sunflower oil. Then add almond milk, molasses, lecithin (or flax meal), raisins, and figs (or dates).

In a separate bowl, sift together the flour, cinnamon, ginger, nutmeg, cloves, orange zest, and baking powder.

Add sifted ingredients to the molasses mixture and combine well with almonds. Pour batter into a well-oiled pudding mold, ¾ full. Seal with a lid.

Steam in a pot half full of hot water for 90 minutes without removing the mold lid. Top up hot water as needed.

Once removed from the steaming pot of water, take the lid off or the pudding will get soggy.

Serve hot with Lemon-Orange Cody.

HINT: Pudding is done when nothing sticks to a tester. If returning to pot, seal lid tight. If you want to reheat the pudding, return to the mold and boil, covered, for 30 minutes.

lemon-orange cody

juice of 2 organic lemons

juice of 1 lime

juice of 3 oranges

1 cup pure maple syrup

2 tbsp arrowroot flour

2 tbsp water

Cody is a traditional Newfoundland sweet sauce used as a coating over duff or pudding.

In a medium saucepan, combine the lemon juice, lime juice, orange juice, and maple syrup and simmer until hot.

Hand mix the arrowroot flour with the water. Then gradually stir the arrowroot mixture into the hot cody.

Serve warm over pudding.

Grandma White's apple pudding

¼ cup sunflower oil

½ cup organic cane sugar

1 tbsp egg replacer mixed with
2 tbsp spring water

1 cup coconut milk

1 cup spelt flour

2 tsp no-alum baking powder

½ tsp pure vanilla

¼ tsp sea salt

1 cup coconut sugar or cane sugar

1½ cups spring water

1 tbsp coconut oil

½ tsp pure vanilla

1 tbsp rice flour mixed with
¼ cup water

6 organic apples, thinly sliced

1 tsp cinnamon

Okay, so maybe Grandma White never made this pudding, but I can picture her conjuring up such a tasty dish in the fall of the year when apples arrived in a barrel from relatives in Nova Scotia. For sure Grandma used spring water!

Preheat oven to 350°F.

In a mixing bowl, whisk together the sunflower oil, organic cane sugar, egg replacer mixed with water, and coconut milk. Then stir in the spelt flour, baking powder, vanilla, and sea salt. Set aside.

In a medium saucepan, combine the coconut sugar, spring water, coconut oil, vanilla, and rice flour mixed with water and bring to a boil for 5 minutes. Reduce heat and simmer while you prepare the apples.

Layer the apple slices over a lightly oiled 12x16-inch baking dish. Sprinkle with cinnamon. Spread batter from the mixing bowl over the apples. Then pour sauce over the batter to cover apples.

Bake for 40 minutes.

3½ cups flour (combination of wheat-free, spelt, and ½ cup coconut flour)

1 tsp no-alum baking powder

1 tsp baking soda

3 tsp cinnamon

2 tsp allspice

½ tsp nutmeg

¼ tsp ground cloves

¾ cup coconut sugar

1 tsp sea salt

2 cups nut milk (coconut or almond)

¾ cup light oil, sunflower or melted coconut

1 tbsp lecithin or flax meal

½ cup chopped walnuts

½ cup chopped almonds

½ cup chopped pecans

1 cup raisins

1 cup currants

1 cup chopped dried organic apricots

zest of 1 orange

zest of 1 lime

juice of 1 orange

juice of 1 lime

irie Christmas fruit cake (1980)

1980 was a good year to make cakes. My friend Ann Doran White and I made 30! Like elves at 4 a.m., we rescued the last four from the oven. Irie is a word some Jamaicans use to describe anything that is created as perfectly as possible.

Preheat oven to 250°F.

In a mixing bowl, combine the flour, baking powder, baking soda, cinnamon, allspice, nutmeg, ground cloves, coconut sugar, and sea salt. Set aside.

In a large mixing bowl, make a buttery mixture by combining the nut milk, light oil, and lecithin (or flax meal). Set aside.

In a third bowl, combine the walnuts, almonds, pecans, raisins, currants, apricots, orange zest, and lime zest. Mix and dust all fruit with a handful of flour. Then pour juice over the fruit.

Combine the fruit and nut mixture with the buttery mixture. Then gradually fold in the spiced flour.

Prepare a 9-inch cast-iron baking pot and lightly oil the bottom. Cut parchment paper to fit the pot and place it in the bottom.

Pour the batter until the pot is ¾ full, smoothing the top.

Bake for 3 hours.

Insert a baking tester in the center to determine if it has cooked all the way to the bottom. If any cake sticks to the tester, bake for an extra 20-30 minutes.

Allow to cool before turning onto a rack.

carrot cake for the ages

2 cups   unsifted all-purpose flour

2 tsp no-alum baking powder

1 tsp baking soda

½ tsp sea salt

2 tsp cinnamon

½ tsp ground ginger

1 tsp powdered nutmeg

1 cup coconut sugar

2 tbsp egg replacer mixed with ¼ cup water

½ cup sunflower oil

1 tsp pure vanilla

1 tsp apple-cider vinegar

½ cup mild flavoured molasses

1 cup finely grated organic carrot

½ cup crushed pineapple

1 cup finely chopped walnuts

½ cup coconut milk

FROSTING

2 cups organic icing sugar

1 cup vegan cream cheese

3 tbsp vegan butter

1 tsp pure vanilla

2 tbsp fresh lemon juice

Preheat oven to 350°F.

In a mixing bowl, combine flour, baking powder, baking soda, sea salt, cinnamon, ginger, nutmeg, and coconut sugar.

In a large measuring cup, combine the egg replacer mixed with water, sunflower oil, vanilla, apple cider vinegar, carrot, pineapple, and ½ cup of walnuts (reserve ½ cup walnuts for the top of the cake).

Gradually add liquid combination to dry ingredients to form a stiff mixture. Let sit for a few minutes to allow carrots to release moisture into the batter.

Add up to ½ cup coconut milk and stir into batter. Then pour into an oiled 9-inch tube pan.

Bake for 40-50 minutes. Remove from oven, let cool for 5 minutes, and turn onto a cooling rack.

TO MAKE THE FROSTING

Stir all of the ingredients by hand until smooth or use an electric mixer. If frosting is too thick, add a few drops of lemon juice; if it's too thin, add more icing sugar or vegan cream cheese.

When cake has cooled, add lots of frosting to the top and sides of the cake. Sprinkle crushed walnuts on top of the cake and serve as soon as possible!

Grandmother Hall's apple cake extraordinaire

1¼ cups all-purpose flour

½ cup pressed coconut sugar

¼ tsp sea salt

1 tsp cinnamon

1 tsp baking soda

2 cups peeled and chopped organic apples

½ cup organic raisins

½ cup fresh squeezed orange juice

1 tsp pure vanilla

1 tbsp egg replacer mixed with ¼ cup water

½ cup sunflower oil

Preheat oven to 350°F.

In a mixing bowl, combine flour, coconut sugar, sea salt, cinnamon, and baking soda. Set aside.

In a separate bowl, combine apples, raisins, orange juice, and vanilla. Set aside.

In a measuring cup, combine the egg replacer mixed with water and the sunflower oil.

Add dry ingredients to the apple mixture. Then mix in the ingredients from the measuring cup until well combined.

Pour into a lightly oiled 8-inch oval pan and bake for 45 minutes.

Test by inserting baking tester into center of cake. Continue to bake 10 more minutes if any cake sticks to the tester.

Anahareo's raisin-nut birthday cake

1 cup raisins

2 tbsp egg replacer mixed with ¼ cup water

1 cup warm coconut milk

1 cup organic coconut sugar

1 tsp pure vanilla

zest of 1 lemon

½ tsp ground anise seed or oil of anise

½ cup avocado oil or melted coconut oil

½ tsp sea salt

2½ cups light flour

3 tsp no-alum baking powder

¼ cup finely chopped walnuts

Soak raisins in ½ cup water for 30 minutes.

Preheat oven to 350°F.

In a blender or food processor, mix the dissolved egg replacer, coconut milk, coconut sugar, vanilla, lemon zest, ground anise seed, avocado oil, and sea salt.

In a mixing bowl, sift together the flour, baking powder, raisins, and raisin water. Then stir these dry ingredients into the wet ingredients. Add walnuts last.

Pour batter into an 8-inch, non-stick, tube cake pan and bake for 35-40 minutes or until a toothpick inserted in the cake comes out clean.

When done, remove from oven and place cake pan on a wire rack to cool for 5 minutes. Then reverse cake pan and continue to cool.

When thoroughly cooled, top with frosting or vegan cream-cheese frosting.

index

Marian Frances White studied journalism at Carleton University and has worked in the Canadian arts scene as a poet, editor, and filmmaker. Marian has been a vegan since the mid-1970s and is the author of *The Eldamar Cookbook: A Fine Vegan Cuisine*. She's worked as a chef and studied at the Hippocrates Heath Institute in Boston. She lives in St. John's.